D1630440

The Small Stream Dry Fly

A New and Radical Approach

By the same author (all published by Swan Hill Press)

Flyfishing Tactics on Small Streams
Trout and Terrestrials
Trout and The Subsurface Fly
The Adaptable Flyfisher
Improve Your Flycasting

The Small Stream Dry Fly

A New and Radical Approach

Lou Stevens

SWAN·HILL
PRESS

Copyright © 2003 Lou Stevens

First published in the UK in 2003
by Swan Hill Press, an imprint of Quiller Publishing Ltd

British Library Cataloguing-in-Publication Data
A catalogue record for this book
is available from the British Library

ISBN 1 904057 24 1

Typeset by Phoenix Typesetting, Burley-in-Wharfedale, West Yorkshire
Printed in England by MPG Books Limited, Bodmin, Cornwall

Swan Hill Press

an imprint of Quiller Publishing Ltd.
Wykey House, Wykey, Shrewsbury, SY4 1JA, England
Tel: 01939 261616 Fax: 01939 261606
E-mail: info@quillerbooks.com
Website:www.swanhillbooks.com

Contents

Figures

Acknowledgement

Without the collaboration of many fine trout this book could never have been written.

Introduction

Whether we fish the dry fly on the chalk streams, hill-streams, brooks, burns or moorland streams, the basic theory is the same. However, the tactics used differ enormously from one type of water to another.

Many excellent books have been written on the dry fly as it pertains to the chalk streams, and the information has been vital in promoting the use of the dry fly on waters of a different type. The use of dry fly is now widely accepted practise on almost all waters, but the chalk stream technique has had to be extensively modified to achieve good results. Perhaps the only real similarity lies in the flies used, and even this similarity is somewhat shattered by the extensive use of terrestrial imitations when fishing small streams.

Although the dry fly is an accepted practise on most waters, efforts must be made to prevent it becoming a cult or an elitist fashion. Certainly, the use of a dry fly on the chalk stream became a cult in its early days, and to a certain extent still is today, although upstream nymph is not considered the heresy it was at one time.

On our type of small stream the exclusive use of a dry fly would be pure affectation. Of course, there are times when the dry fly will outfish all other methods, but such times are few and far between. Studies have shown that trout obtain between 75 and 85 per cent of their food subsurface. It would be a foolish person indeed who continued to use a dry fly regardless of conditions that dictated otherwise.

On the other hand there is something utterly delightful and intriguing in taking a trout on a dry fly, especially a fly that has been tied, (and perhaps evolved), by the angler personally. Many pursue the use of a dry fly when they know it is useless to do so, and that another tactic would bring better results. Such a person can't be classified as foolish if they knowingly determine to do what gives them the greatest pleasure, the result is not the criteria.

In the following pages we will try to keep our feet firmly on the ground and adopt tactics that will result in banked fish.

Let us first discuss the variety of the waters that so influence the tactics we use . . .

1

The Water We Fish

The Small Rain-Fed Stream

The small rain-fed stream may be one of several types. Sometimes it is a hillstream in its own right, at other times it may be a tributary of a major river, or even a tributary of a tributary. It may flow at a fast pace down steep hillsides and become rock strewn in the process, it may, on the other hand, be a placid stream through lowland pastures, or, alternatively, wend its way through a heavily wooded valley and have overgrown banks.

The stream bed may be rocky, of fine gravel, or perhaps made up of a combination of silt and mud. In many cases the clarity of the water is dependent on the terrain through which the stream flows.

The water of the hillstream will probably be on the acid side (pH value 4 to 6.8), and as a result the trout will often be generally small and highly coloured. However, it must not be supposed that all hillstream trout are small, there are always exceptions!

One thing all these stream types have in common is that they are severely affected by rain. They rely directly on rainfall for their water flow and level, and consequently there is often a feast or famine of water flow depending on the season and the weather.

At times of heavy or prolonged rain many of these streams can become raging torrents, and it can happen very suddenly depending on the terrain. Other streams,

The centre rock creates two 'Change of Pace' zones. See Appendix 'A' (1 and 4)

This hillstream has many 'Change of Pace' zones. See Appendix 'A' (7)

perhaps through lowland pasture, can also rise considerably, sometimes overflowing their banks, and are often
very muddy and coloured.

The periods of intense water flow have the effect of
scouring the stream bed, displacing plant life, destroying
a quantity of nymphal forms of insect life and sometimes
laying down fresh silt. Banks are frequently undercut and
regular trout lies sometimes destroyed and new ones
created.

During times of drought, and even during high summer,
water flows diminish. The streams become low, and in
some cases almost dry up. Every part of the stream
becomes miniaturised with the water crystal clear.

The effect of these rain, (or lack of rain), induced
changes are nearly always the same. As we have seen, the
unfiltered water coming directly from the surrounding
terrain is usually acid, which does little to induce underwater plant life. Whatever plant life does get a hold is
often very sparse.

Lack of plant life results in a decrease of nymphal insect
life, in fact small underwater life in general, and consequently fly hatches become sparse and irregular. Fish
thrive and grow depending, among other things, on the
food supply available, and therefore are often small and
hungry.

During times of heavy rain, food for the fish, for
example worms, grubs, ants, beetles etc., is washed into
the stream. During times of drought the fish have to rely
on opportunistic feeding. All in all it is not an ideal
habitat for sustained fish growth.

The Limestone Stream

Limestone streams, (which our American cousins call
spring creeks), very often have the general appearance of

a rain-fed river, but nearly always the tell-tale signs of its limestone origins can be seen.

The typical limestone river runs through, or has its source in, the limestone hills. During periods of heavy rain the surrounding porous limestone terrain absorbs much of the rainfall and only a moderate amount of water runs off the land into the stream. Rain permiates the limestone terrain, very often into underground caves, and enters the river by way of springs. Such spring water has been filtered through the limestone over a long period of time and has become alkaline (pH 7.6 to 8.4), in the process.

It is true that limestone streams do rise during and after rain. However, the rise is mostly the result of increased water flow from the springs and is usually on the moderate side.

It is the alkaline nature of the water plus the fairly consistent water flow from the springs, that create the character of the limestone river.

Like its close relative, the chalk stream, the limestone river is rich in plant life. Consequently underwater animal and insect larval forms thrive and flourish. The trout, likewise, thrive and grow on the abundant food supply. Hatches of aquatic fly are frequent, but not to the extent of the chalk stream where the stream flow is more placid.

The limestone river trout is a robust fish, and good size fish can be expected as a result of the fairly easy living conditions.

Lowland Water

Lowland waters can, again, be of various types. It may well be that a hillstream becomes a lowland water as its lower reaches meander through a deep valley. A common feature of such valley streams is overgrown banks that nearly hide the water. In contrast are the moorland streams that make their way through an almost barren landscape, often with a rocky and boulder-strewn water course. The term 'pocket water', which is often heard in the USA, aptly describes the little, (almost tiny), pools between the scattered rocks.

Another example of lowland water is the meadow or pastureland stream. Although very different from the moorland or valley stream, it may, nevertheless, be good trout habitat. Such waters very often have a good head of coarse fish such as chub, roach and dace. Trout, in fact good size well fed trout, are also often present. It is a fact that as trout grow larger and greater quantities of food are required, they often drop downstream to take up permanent lies in lowland water.

Summary

We must, of course, bear in mind that many waters are combinations of the various types mentioned and cannot really be placed in any definite category.

The one common factor is that they are not chalk streams and do not lend themselves to chalk stream fishing techniques and tactics.

The trout, themselves, also vary in characteristics from stream to stream. The small super-active trout of the hill and moorland stream require a very different approach to the tactics that are successful on the limestone rivers.

Without doubt the dry fly angler on small streams has to be very versatile and be prepared to vary the tactics used. The ability to 'read a stream' is of paramount importance, and knowledge of small stream insect life including terrestrials needs to be honed to a fine point.

Let us now have a discussion on tackle innovations . . .

2

Tackle Innovations

The Tackle We Use

A discussion on a range of tackle in detail would make rather boring reading when we are only considering one aspect of our sport, that of fishing the dry fly.

General books on flyfishing usually cover the question of tackle quite fully, and, of course, advice can be obtained from tackle suppliers. However, be warned, just because a person is a tackle dealer does not mean that he or she is a 'Tackle Guru' whose advice can be slavishly followed. Only too often the advice given is aimed to sell what is advantageous to the dealership. When seeking such advice it is best if it is obtained from one of the leading tackle houses.

Here we are going to discuss only those items of tackle, and their modification, which particularly appertain to fishing the dry fly on small streams. We will also discuss the 'rigging' of such tackle where special 'rigs' are advantageous to us.

Flylines

Without doubt the finest dry-fly line – for practical fishing – that was ever produced was the Double Taper Dressed Silk Line, even if it was an infernal nuisance to maintain. Practically all flyfishers today use plastic lines of one type or another.

However, we must not be confused by the intense sales hype of the manufacturers who would have us believe that their particular line has reached the very pinnacle of performance. Lines *serve* the flyfisher, only flyfishers *perform*!

We should grade a flyline by its closeness in action to a top grade silk line – that is the standard we strive for. Of course, the line needs to have all the required standard features. It should be, or is best to have, a double taper profile, it should float well, even at the extreme tip. It should be supple with almost no built-in 'memory', and there should be a long gradual front taper ending in a fine tip.

In the USA the weight-forward line is commonly used when fishing the dry fly. We are told over and over again in sales hype that with a short line in use the weight-forward line performs identically to a double taper. It is just not so. The front taper of a weight-forward line is generally too short and heavy compared to a good double taper profile.

Almost all plastic lines are made of PVC, (polyvinyl chloride), but a few manufacturers are using polyurethane. In the past polyurethane lines have been plagued with 'memory' problems, the lines have separated from their core when a nail-knot has been used to secure a leader, and the tips have been too large in diameter. However, today most of the early difficulties have been overcome.

The polyurethane line has the advantage of a harder-wearing surface, it is very nearly crack proof and requires almost no dressing from the angler to maintain the suppleness of the line. However, the tip of the line is usually of a larger diameter than a comparable PVC line and does not land on the water with the same finesse. Also, polyurethane does not seem to tolerate cold conditions or cold water as well as PVC, and stiffness and 'memory' can become problems.

The plastic flyline normally has a braided synthetic core, usually of Dacron. Today some flylines are being manufactured with monofilament cores, (monofilament nylon), and such lines present us with certain difficulties.

At a later stage we are going to discuss attaching the leader to the flyline. Be warned, mono-core lines completely destroy our recommended strategy. If you use a mono-core line the procedure will have to be entirely different.

If you have, or can acquire, an engineer's micrometer, you will find it one of the most useful items in your flyfishing kit. Very often a second-hand micrometer can be purchased from a market stall very cheaply and learning how to use it takes only a few minutes. Consider how useful it would be to be able to measure accurately the diameters of flylines, the tapers of flylines, nylon leaders and tippet materials.

Rigging the Flyline

Having acquired a flyline the next step is to attach a leader. (See Fig.1.) There are several ways to do this:

1. Tie the flyline by a 'figure of eight' knot to a loop in the leader butt (not illustrated).

2. Tie the leader to the end of the flyline by means of a nail-knot.

3. Pass the leader butt up into the flyline tip, then out of the side of the flyline and finish with a nail-knot round the line.

4. Use a plastic cast connector.

5. Use an eyed metal barbed connector.

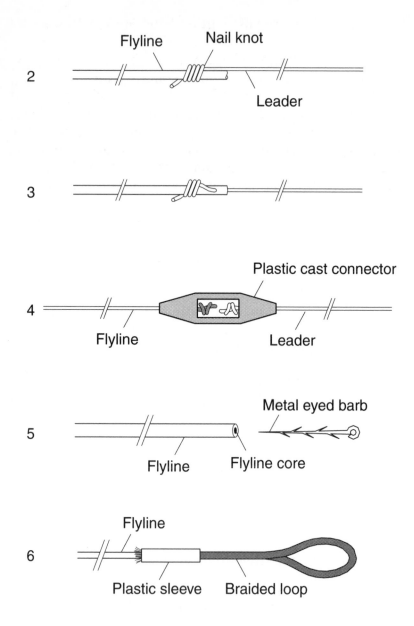

Fig. 1   Leader to Flyline Connections

6. Fit a braided loop to the end of the flyline by means of a sleeve and connect to the leader by 'loop to loop'.

7. Form a flyline core loop and attach leader by 'loop to loop' (not illustrated).

What a quandary! Let us try and simplify things. No.1 is the old tried and tested method when silk lines were in general use and is not recommended for plastic lines. No.2 is commonly used by reservoir/stillwater flyfishers. It is crude but effective when using heavy lures and flies and finesse is not the criteria. No.3 is a neater variation of No.2 but is still a little crude. No.4 at first sight appears to be a dream solution. However, in use the little plastic connector is often cracked when passing through the tip ring of the rod. The result is a sudden parting between flyline and leader. No.5 is an old fashioned version of No.4, more secure but by its nature causes a 'hinge' action between flyline and leader. No.6 is the most used method today. It is very effective but has the great disadvantage of thickening the flyline tip – something we have taken great pains to advocate against. No.7 is definitely our recommendation for dry fly fishing.

Forming a Flyline Core Loop
The procedure for forming a flyline loop is not easy to explain using only words, it becomes a lot easier when the line-drawing sequence is followed. See Fig.2.

(a) Remove about 4in of line coating from the braided core at the line tip. The easiest way is to dip the tip in Flyline Coating Remover for about five minutes. (Obtainable from Sport Fish, Winforton, nr. Hereford, HR3 6SP, UK.)

(b) Fray out about 1in of the core tip, divide in half and snip off one half of the fray.

11

The Small Stream Dry Fly

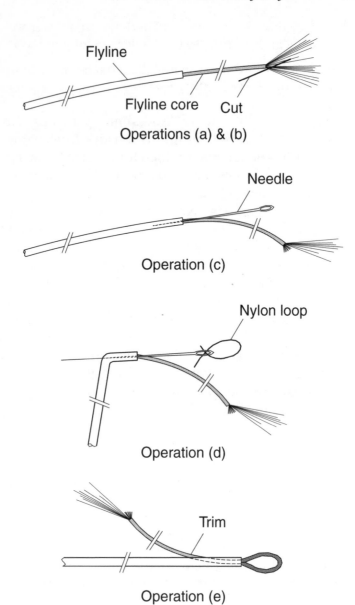

Flyline

Flyline core   Cut

Operations (a) & (b)

Needle

Operation (c)

Nylon loop

Operation (d)

Trim

Operation (e)

Fig. 2   A Line Loop

(c) Pass a sharp needle (about .015in dia) up into the core of the flyline commencing where the flyline coating starts. After entering about ½in stop.

(d) Run a loop of 3x nylon through the needle eye, pull the needle out through the side of the flyline leaving the nylon loop exposed.

(e) Insert the half frayed tip of the core into the nylon loop. Pull into the flyline and out of the side carrying the core through at the same time to form a loop. Trim off flush with flyline.

Note: For safety apply a tiny drop of superglue to the core just before pulling into the flyline.

The result of this seemingly (but not really) difficult operation, is the neatest flyline loop you will ever see and the flyline tip diameter is almost unchanged.

Leaders

The recommendation for dry fly fishing on small streams is a 12ft leader. This may sound a bit too dogmatic, but it is not really so. When our tactics are discussed in detail it will be seen that such a leader fulfils our needs in nearly all situations.

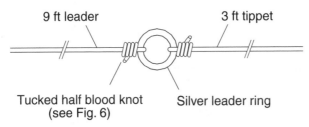

9 ft leader   3 ft tippet

Tucked half blood knot (see Fig. 6)   Silver leader ring

Fig. 3   The Leader Ring

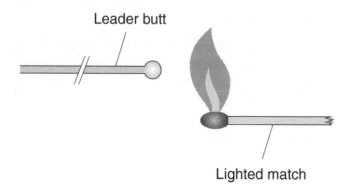

Leader butt

Lighted match

Fig. 4   The Leader Butt

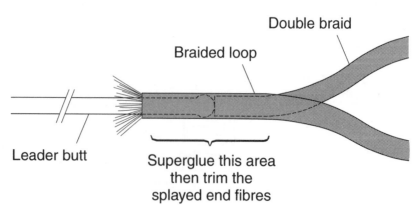

Double braid

Braided loop

Leader butt

Superglue this area
then trim the
splayed end fibres

Fig. 5   The Leader Loop

Tackle Innovations

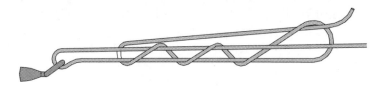

The Pitzenknot

(a) Fold the tippet double well away from the fly
(b) Wind the tippet three times back towards the fly
(c) Pass the tippet back through the loop as shown
(d) Pull knot half tight
(e) Pull knot up to fly and watch for the turnover on the fly head

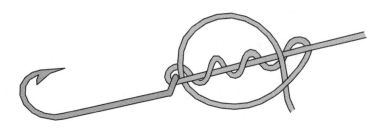

Tucked Half Blood Knot

Fig. 6   Nylon Knots

The Small Stream Dry Fly

If a 9ft standard 3x (.008in dia tip) leader is purchased and then a tiny silver leader ring tied securely to the tip, a 3ft tippet of 4x or 5x nylon can be attached to complete our 12ft leader. If a break-off is ever necessary because of being caught up in weeds, trees etc., the leader plus tip ring are normally undamaged. Only a new tippet is required. See Figs 3 and 6.

Now we have to consider the leader to flyline connection. We need a connection that will create (1) a loop to loop connection with the loop already created at the tip of our flyline, and (2) that will be a slim connection that is almost a continuation of the flyline diameter and will enable the flyline tip to land on the water with the minimum of disturbance. Also (3) it must create a join that does not allow the flyline/leader connection to 'hinge' during the casting process.

I suggest a 'braided loop' at the butt of the leader, and to join it to the leader in the following manner.

Any knotted nylon loop at the butt of the leader should be trimmed off. The butt can now be held close to, but not touching, a lighted match. Immediately the nylon butt forms a slight bulge, remove from the heat. See Fig. 4. Now pass the butt of the leader up into the standing braid of the braided loop until it touches the double braid of the loop. Place a small drop of superglue on the connection and trim off surplus braid from the butt of the leader. See Fig. 5.

It may sound a lot of work but the description takes longer to read than actually doing the job which is quite easy. All the effort will have been very worthwhile for you now have a first class flyline/leader where the leader or tippet can be changed at any time and the actual connection is almost part of the flyline. The utmost finesse in presentation is now possible.

Leader to Fly

We are still considering tackle in the light of presenting a dry fly. True, the leader to fly connection can hardly be considered as 'tackle', but the knot used is of the utmost importance and is part of the equipment we use.

Years ago the 'turle knot' was widely used for the dry fly. It was a good secure knot that allowed the dry fly to be held steady and in line with the leader. Today the knot is rarely used. The advent of nylon superseded many knots that were only ideal for gut. In addition the still-water flyfisher found a 'tucked half blood knot' served him very well for heavier flies and lures.

There is no doubt that the 'turle knot' is difficult to tie well when using a fine nylon tippet, also the fine nylon loop is inclined to catch in the fly dressing when pulled tight. Nevertheless we do require the advantages of a 'turle knot', so we must find another way.

Using a 'tucked half blood knot' for a dry fly is very unsatisfactory. Many fish are lost, or put down, by a dry fly that is badly cocked on the water caused by the fly being 'hinged' at the knot. It is essential that the fly is held in line with the tippet and is nicely 'cocked' on the water.

An easy way out of our dilemma is to use a 'pitzenknot'. This knot is not widely known in the UK, but its advantage is that it almost ties a 'turle knot' from the *front* of the fly. It is well worth the time spent learning it. See Fig. 6.

General

We have not discussed rods, reels, landing nets and the multitude of items that go to make up the flyfisher's tackle. This has been deliberate as these items are a

Between the weedbeds are many 'Change of Pace' zones. See Appendix 'A' (3)

matter of personal choice and it is assumed that our reader already has his/her own personal preferences. It is worth repeating again that we are considering only one aspect of our beloved sport and only what will help us to fish a dry fly successfully on a small stream.

However, before we proceed much further we will need to discuss the leader itself in greater depth . . .

3

Leaders

In the previous chapter under the sub-heading 'Leaders' we referred to a standard 9ft leader with a 3x tip. Such a leader requires considerable discussion for there are so many different 'standard' leaders made of many different materials. All have their uses, all have their own individual characteristics.

Over the years my views on leaders have changed considerably. At one time I was prepared to advocate braided leaders over all others, now a little older and wiser I am prepared to listen to all sides of the debate.

I can do no greater service to the reader than attempt to lay out a comprehensive review of the main types of leader available. Perhaps out of such a review enough information will be gleaned for an opinion to be formed. Firstly we need to consider the various types of leader that are available . . .

Mono-leaders

Mono-leaders are single filament leaders, but the filament may be made of a variety of different materials.

Nylon monofilament in various forms is the most commonly used, and the resulting leader may vary from soft/supple to very stiff over a wide range. Opinions as to which is best are often influenced by the old traditions associated with the period when natural silk-worm gut was in use. Silk-worm gut was a stiff, brittle substance that could be softened to varying degrees by soaking in water.

Without doubt the 'perfect' leader would be stiff in the butt, so as to aid turnover, and becoming soft and supple at the tippet to aid presentation and to reduce drag. Unfortunately the manufactured mono-leader does not give us such a choice.

Another nylon-type material used commercially is Copolymer. Such leaders are manufactured from resin-impregnated copolymide, often double stretched. The result is a stiffer leader that could be classed as 'double strength'. Straightening is rather troublesome compared to soft nylon, but a swift rub-down with a piece of rubber usually cures the problem. A decided advantage is the greater breaking strain for a given diameter.

A new innovation is the fluorocarbon leader. These leaders are somewhat expensive, as is all fluorocarbon. The advantages are claimed to be (1) a zero water absorbency, (2) a refractive index close to that of water resulting in invisibility, and (3) a specific gravity of approximately 1.78 that results in the material sinking through the water surface film. In addition fluorocarbon is usually on the stiff side when compared to standard monofilament.

The claimed advantages need to be evaluated by the reader. Zero water absorbency is a debatable feature, the claimed higher specific gravity is a plus feature, but fine tippets under 3x (.008in) are almost impossible to sink no matter what the material. Of course, we all desire invisibility, but total invisibility is just not available under any circumstances.

All this discourse leads us to consider what the dimensional specification should be of a good mono-leader.

Firstly, we are satisfied that it should be tapered, but between what diameters? Also should it be a continuous taper or stepped tapers?

The average tip diameter of a good quality flyline usually lies between .033in and .038in, and it is essential to good turnover that the butt diameter of a mono-leader be approximately two-thirds of this, i.e. .020in to .025in, depending on the stiffness of the material. In several mail order catalogues such leaders are sometimes referred to as 'Big-Butt-Leaders'. The small diameter butt (.015in) found on so many commercially made mono-leaders is a throwback to the times of silk-worm gut leaders and the very thin-tipped silk lines that were in use at the time.

Many commercially made mono-leaders have a continuous taper from butt to tip. For dry fly fishing this is poor mono-leader construction and is usually associated with the small-butt type of leader.

The recommended construction for a dry fly leader that will give a controlled turnover is approximately as shown in Fig.7. Of course, these specifications are not set in stone, but they give a very good indication of what we should look for.

One way we can have exactly what we want is to make up our own leaders by knotting together lengths of various diameter nylon. See Fig.8.

However a few words of warning:

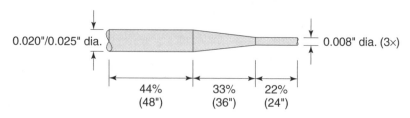

Fig. 7   Leader Dimensional Profile

Leaders

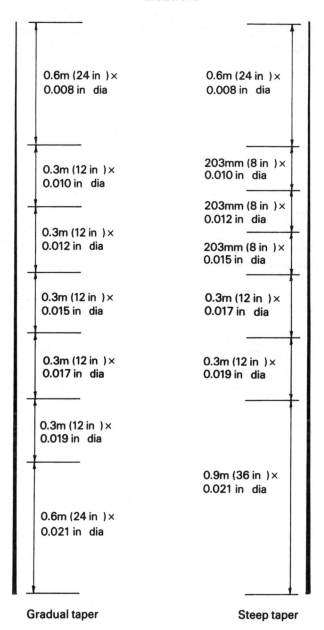

0.6m (24 in) ×
0.008 in dia

0.3m (12 in) ×
0.010 in dia

0.3m (12 in) ×
0.012 in dia

0.3m (12 in) ×
0.015 in dia

0.3m (12 in) ×
0.017 in dia

0.3m (12 in) ×
0.019 in dia

0.6m (24 in) ×
0.021 in dia

Gradual taper

0.6m (24 in) ×
0.008 in dia

203mm (8 in) ×
0.010 in dia

203mm (8 in) ×
0.012 in dia

203mm (8 in) ×
0.015 in dia

0.3m (12 in) ×
0.017 in dia

0.3m (12 in) ×
0.019 in dia

0.9m (36 in) ×
0.021 in dia

Steep taper

Fig. 8   Home-tied Leaders

23

1. Always use lengths of nylon that are of the same make and type.

2. Never tie together two strands of nylon that vary in diameter more than .002in.

3. Use blood-knots or surgeon-knots to join the strands – and tie them with care.

Tying your own used to be the very best way to make leaders. Today it is possible to buy commercial leaders that are tapered in the correct manner and are made in the material of our choice. They are expensive compared to the cost of homemade leaders, which are often a labour of love. However, we do have a choice.

Polyleaders

We are now being offered commercial polyleaders consisting of a mono-nylon core coated with polymer to form a short, (usually 5ft), tapered leader. The idea is to create a smooth transition of power from line to leader, to which can be added a tippet of personal choice. A claimed advantage is that polymer can be factory colour-coded and treated to float, or to sink at varying rates.

The power transmission from line to leader is first class, and the various densities are without doubt an advantage to the stillwater flyfisher. The river angler will be more concerned with the abnormal tippet length required and the lack of finesse in the fly presentation due to the weight of the polymer. It must be understood that basically the leader becomes an extension of the flyline terminating in an overlength level tippet. The manufacturers claim that up to 12ft of 2lb level tippet can be added. So, the final effect for the river flyfisherman could well be that of a flyline extended by 5ft of polymer

tapered leader terminating in 7 to 8ft of 2lb level monofilament tippet. Well . . . 'You pays yer money and takes yer
choice!'

Braided Leaders

As previously pointed out, at one time I was of the opinion
that the ultimate had been achieved with the introduc-
tion of braided leaders. The original leaders were akin to
plaited rope, but progress was quickly made and useable
leaders were very soon generally available.

It would seem that the UK were pioneers in this process,
but in the early years Spain and Austria made the most
rapid progress. It was the Spanish leaders that I was so
enthusiastic about in those early days.

As time went by it became very apparent that a 5ft
braided leader with a 4ft nylon tippet attached was,
firstly, not long enough to give a really good fly presentation and secondly, on lifting off line to recast spray from
the woven braid was far too close to the fly, (i.e. the tippet
length of 4ft). It was then that braided leaders of 8ft, 10ft
and 12ft began to be available.

At first sight the problem appeared solved, but it was
not so. Finesse in presentation was more easily achieved
with the longer leader, but only on still and windless days.
At the very slightest hint of a breeze the long very supple
light braid behaved with a devilish mind of its own.

To sum up, the braided leader produced a smooth transition of power from line to leader with wonderfully
controlled turnover, but the short length leader caused
spray and disturbance on lift-off. The longer length
leaders improved finesse but were uncontrollable in any
wind.

As previously said, I am no longer wedded to braided
leaders. However, I still prefer them to the poly leaders

when any type of sinking model is required, for instance, when fishing nymphs or emergers, but they no longer suit me for generally fishing the dry fly.

Before we actually fish together we need to discuss briefly the flies needed for small streams . . .

4

The Small Stream Flybox

The chalk stream flyfisher, rod in hand, patiently concentrating on looking for a rising fish, is a mental picture we are all familiar with.

The chalk stream rules that usually only rising fish may be cast to, and that the presentation be made by an upstream cast using a dry fly or nymph, may seem very archaic to a small stream angler. However, the prolific fly life of the chalk stream together with the outstanding and regular fly hatches, results in a trout population that are confirmed surface feeders. Under such circumstances it is not difficult to appreciate that flyfishing can be preserved in its most elite form. Certainly, prospecting likely trout lies by fishing a wet fly downstream would be classified as 'cowboy' behaviour of the worst kind, and prospecting with a dry fly not that much better. Just not the activities of 'gentlemen'!

Fishing a dry fly on our small streams has almost nothing in common with the above. True, we look for rising fish whenever we can. After all a rising fish is a feeding fish, and a feeding fish is half the equation of a fish in the bag.

Most small streams, (perhaps certain limestone streams may be excepted), do not have prolific hatches of fly. They almost certainly do have *some* sporadic hatches but almost never on the scale of the chalk streams. The reasons for this state of affairs have been previously discussed in Chapter 1, and it is extremely difficult to see any change in the future.

Often the angler will see several flies over the water and with luck one or two rises to them, but a hatch resulting in a flotilla of floating duns . . . hardly ever.

It has often been noted that the flies over the water are mating spinners and that the rises seen are to spent spinners that are floating in the surface film. The actual hatch has been so sporadic and short-lived that we have not even seen or noticed it.

However, our fish – ever the opportunistic feeders – will often rise to a tasty morsel, including our artificial if it is well presented.

We must use our river craft to search out likely fish lies and present our fly correctly to such places. When a rising fish is seen it is indeed a welcome bonus.

Most flyfishers carry far too many different varieties of flies. It is not uncommon to see a flybox crammed with up to 60 different flies, sometimes even over 100 in total. If a survey is made of such a box it will usually be found that only 8 to 12 flies are regularly used depending on the water fished. The remainder are 'desperation flies' to be used when everything else has failed and are consequently rarely successful. It would be far better to bring the collection down to a workable level and to make sure that the flies chosen are available in three sizes. The recommendation for the UK is sizes 14, 16 and 18 which best correspond to natural fly sizes.

Regarding which flies should make up such a reduced flybox, the information previously written in my book *The Adaptable Flyfisher*, (Swan Hill Press), is hard to improve upon and is quoted below . . .

It is of considerable help to the angler when trying to identify natural flies if he has a fair idea of what may be expected at

The bridge across the stream creates a 'Change of Pace' zone. See Appendix 'A' (6)

various times of the day or season. Even if flies are not apparent and general prospecting is in order, it still helps if the artificial selected matches the fly that might be expected by the fish. Fish are often selective while a hatch is actually taking place, and at that time it is essential to use the correct artificial. Even when there is no hatch, fish are inclined to be wary of fly patterns that have no place on the water at that time. They may not associate with food artificials that bear no resemblance to the flies recently seen.

It would be impossible to specify the particular fly that could be on the water at a certain time of the day, or during a particular part of the season. Fly hatches are influenced by water and air temperatures, weather pressure systems, and whether the day is bright or dull, cold or windy. There is also a considerable overlapping between species. However, the following, if taken in a general sense, might be a useful guide.

Very early in the season, when it is often quite cold, fly hatches, (in fact any form of fly life), are not that common. However, even in quite cold weather the march brown will appear. This is one of our very large flies and easy to identify with its brown body and fawn-coloured wings. At such times, prospecting with a dry fly is not very rewarding, and the use of terrestrial patterns is almost useless. It is a different matter during a hatch of march browns, and good sport will often result. The hatches are usually of a short duration, but several may occur during the midday period.

April brings some improvement. March browns may still be encountered, and this is the month of the large dark olive. This insect is also easy to identify due to its dark olive-coloured body. It has smoky blue-grey wings and is quite large. Hatches are inclined to be more prolific than with the march brown, and again take place during the midday period. Fish at this time of the year are normally lean and hungry and the hatches of large olives are greedily attacked. The grannom and silver sedge also make their appearance at this time of the year, and a few medium olives may be expected.

During the early spring, march browns become rare, large dark olives are still encountered, but it is time for the medium olive. This is a smaller fly than the large olive, and is usually lighter olive in colour, but colours vary enormously from water to water, and sometimes between flies. Grannom, silver sedge and black gnats are also evident at this time of the year.

May will bring the hatches of iron blues, especially if the weather is cold. When examined closely, the iron blue's name is clearly accurate, but from a distance the fly appears to be almost black. Olives are still on the water, particularly the medium olive, and during the evening sedges will appear, especially at dusk. Black gnats become more plentiful, and if the weather is warm a few pale wateries may be seen late in the day.

The summer months begin to bring an end to the midday hatches. Iron blues and olives are still inclined to hatch on colder days, but not to the same extent, and pale wateries will now be more obvious. Sedges are also plentiful in early evening. Spinners are over the water laying eggs during the day, and rising fish may well be taking 'spent' spinners from the water surface. Most hatches are now taking place during the early evening and terrestrials are quite plentiful.

The tail of the season brings the return of black gnats, sometimes in gigantic numbers. Olives and pale wateries are still about, although during the day it may well be the 'spent' spinner that attracts interest. Towards the very end of the season large dark olives may reappear, especially if there is a decided drop in temperature. Generally speaking, flies are not that abundant, but fish are quite active and prospecting likely lies brings good results.

Now comes the difficult task of selecting artificials to represent these natural flies – there are so many patterns to choose from. The list in Fig.9 may help establish a basic fly box to which the angler can add as time goes by.

Terrestrials are by far the main food of trout during high summer. Very often it is advisable during the middle part of the day to concentrate our efforts on fishing dry terrestrial patterns. An induced rise is much more likely to a deer-hair beetle than to an orthodox fly. This is particularly true when fishing trout lies that are close to the

Natural	Artificial
Large dark olive	Dark Olive, Blue Upright, Gold-ribbed Hare's Ear (Spinner: Large Red Spinner)
Medium olive	Medium Olive, Rough Olive, Gold-ribbed Hare's Ear, Greenwell's Glory (Spinner: Lunn's Particular)
Blue-winged olive	Blue-Winged Olive (Spinner: Sherry Spinner)
Pale wateries	Tup's Indispensable, Blue Quill, Pale Watery (Spinner: Amber Spinner)
Iron blues	Iron Blue (Spinner: Houghton Ruby or Jenny Spinner)
March brown	March Brown (Spinner: a much lighter-coloured fly)
Sedges	Brown Sedge, Silver Sedge, Welshman's Button.
Alders Willow flies Black gnats	Standard patterns

Fig. 9   Natural flies and their imitation

bank and heavily overgrown. A few suitable patterns are shown in Figs. 10, 11, and 12. See also my book *Trout and Terrestrials*, (Swan Hill Press).

Now that we have our tackle sorted out and our flybox well primed, let us go fishing . . .

GREEN CATERPILLAR

Hook : 10 or 12 extra long shank
Body : Light green chenille
Head : Peacock herl

BLACK CATERPILLAR

Hook : 10 or 12 extra long shank
Body : Black ostrich herl
Head : Peacock herl

Fig. 10   Terrestrial Patterns

ANT

Hook   : 10, 12, 14 or 16 long shank
Body   : Two segments of body plus head
are built up with black tying silk,
then given several coats of lacquer
until glossy
Hackle : Black

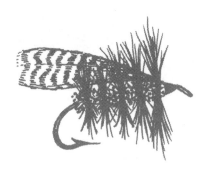

NIGHT MOTH

Hook   : 10 or 12 long shank
Body   : Deer hair (spun Muddler Minnow style)
clipped very short
Wing   : Duck or teal breast feather fibres
Hackle : Brown – tied palmer

Fig. 11   Terrestrial Patterns

DADDY-LONG-LEGS

Hook   : 12 or 14 extra long shank
Body   : Strands of deer hair bound along
               hook and shank to beyond the bend, cut
               off square
Wings : Brown hackle points
Legs   : Pheasant tail fibres knotted, tied-in
               so as lie straight back
Hackle : Brown

DRONE FLY

Hook   : 10, 12 or 14 long shank
Rear body : Built up with black and yellow
                tying silk, then lacquered until
                glossy
Front body: Built up with black tying silk,
                then lacquered until glossy
Hackle   : Brown

Fig. 12   Terrestrial Patterns

5

Dry Fly Tactics (1)

Our first fishing session together will be on a small hill-stream in South Wales. It is not a fictitious stream, it is one that I have fished on a regular basis for a number of years. It is, in fact, a tributary of a famous river and our first session together will be on the upper reaches some twelve miles above the confluence.

The stream is a typical rain-fed hillstream, slightly acid and very rocky with a series of good small pools. Underwater plant life is on the sparse side and the banks can be high and overgrown in places. The water is always slightly coloured, a better description would be a light whisky shade but usually quite clear. The trout are definitely on the small side, 'three to the pound' is a good description, but there is always the chance of a larger fish.

During periods of heavy rain this stream becomes a raging torrent, one year it even destroyed a solid stone bridge downstream. However, today is a typical early spring day, the water is in reasonable condition and the weak watery sun on the water will be helpful to us.

Before we commence activities we need to study the situation in detail. At this time of the year we might expect to see a few large olives about, but fly life on this stream is a trifle spasmodic and unreliable to say the least. We would be in for a long spell of inactivity if we were to sit on the bank and wait for a hatch to develop. We may see the odd rise if we are lucky, but we certainly cannot rely on that. Nevertheless, we do have an important fact in our favour, the fish in this stream are always hungry and on the look-out for food. The water is generally shallow enough that they will rise freely to surface food, and that includes our fly if it is correctly presented.

We must read the water and look for likely trout lies such as shown in Figs. 13 and 14, and present our fly to such places so that we obtain a drag-free float over the lie. See Fig.15.

We must always remember a simple rule, which I call the 'change of pace rule'. This states that trout normally lie close to where the pace of the current changes to a slower tempo. Trout love to be close to a good current flow that brings food to them like a conveyor belt, but they need to be in a slower flow that is adjacent to the main current so that their energy is conserved. Such a lie enables them to move into the main current flow as and when a tasty morsel presents itself. So we must look for trout lies that conform to the 'change of pace rule'. Slack water by the side of the main current, slower water close to the stream bank, water downstream of a submerged rock etc., all such trout lies conform to the 'change of pace rule'. See Figs. 13 and 14. At the same time we must keep an eye open for any rises that will give away the lie of a fish, we might also be able to locate fish by sight if we search the water diligently. Polaroid glasses are a great help in this respect and also offer us eye protection when casting.

We must now consider what fly to use. As described previously in Chapter 4, it is early spring and large olives could normally be expected, but today none are to be seen. On some streams the march browns might hatch at this time of the year, but again none are apparent.

Terrestrials do not form a major part of the trout diet in early spring, but some terrestrials such as beetles do find

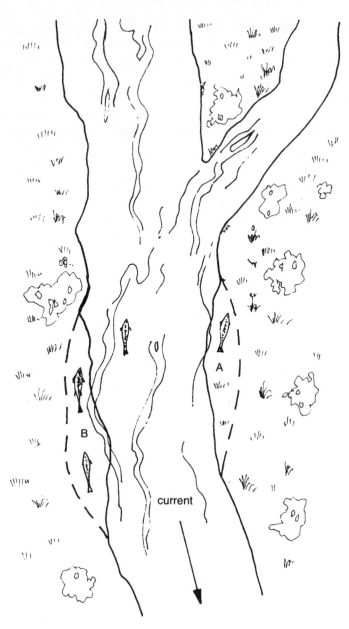

Fig. 13   'Change of Pace' zones

themselves on the water by accident. Leaf hoppers among the new leaf growth can also fall on the water from over-hanging foliage.

Our choice is therefore one of three options. (1) Use a large olive imitation such as a Greenwell's Glory or Gold Ribbed Hare's Ear, on the grounds that the fish may expect to see such a fly, or (2) use a beetle imitation such as a 'deer hair' beetle to induce a rise, or (3) use a small green coloured wet fly that has been treated with floatant so as to float and imitate a fallen leaf hopper on the surface. The latter option is a last resort trick that very often works when all else has failed.

It would be a good idea to start operations in a con-ventional manner and put up a Greenwell's Glory, – we can change flies if we get a poor response. Our fly should be on the large side this early in the season, ideally size 14.

We can see that the current in front of us is very much in mid-stream leaving the water under the far bank moving at a slower pace. It fits our 'change of pace rule' very well, but the problem will be casting a line across the fast current.

A line or leader cast across a fast current will be taken up by that current and cause any fly on slower water to 'drag'. 'Drag' may be defined as an unnatural movement of the fly caused by a pull on the line or leader by a faster current of water. The drag may be severe or almost imper-ceptible, the result is almost always the same . . . *no trout in his right mind will touch the fly!*

So, we have to avoid drag, which is almost impossible, but we must try. There are several ways to reduce drag and as our skills improve we will find more and more ways, but basically all methods are intended to produce a similar result, that is to say they aim to avoid casting a straight line that can be acted upon immediately by the current.

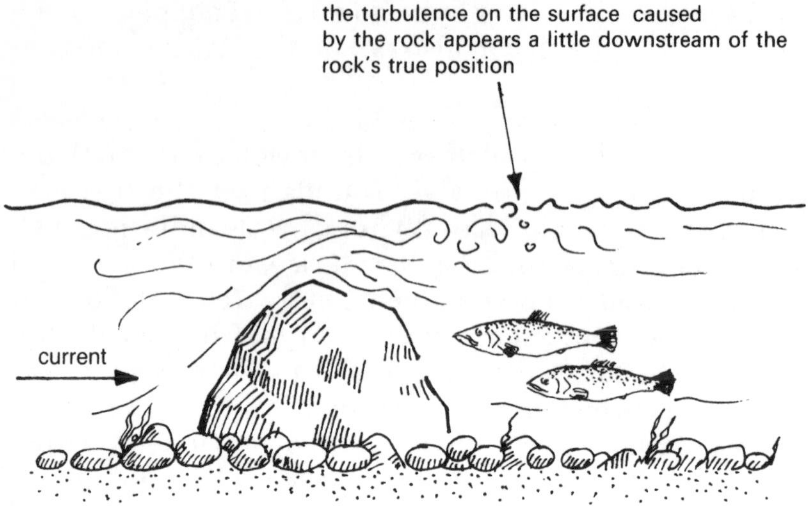

the turbulence on the surface caused by the rock appears a little downstream of the rock's true position

current

Fig. 14   The Streambed Rock

We can fish a fly close to that far bank with a minimum of drag if we cast the fly upstream and adopt the following procedure.

False cast a couple of times to measure the distance, but on the second or third false cast put out an additional 3 or 4ft of line. On the final forward cast as the line unfurls in front quickly wiggle the rod tip from side to side so that the line descends to the water in a series of 'S' shaped curves. It is a very easy thing to do and the curves take up the additional length of line that you added into the cast. The fly lands on the target area to which it was aimed and has a drag-free float until the current has straightened out the curves in the line. Let us now give it a try . . .

Well, our strategy worked and brought very good results. In working the fly along the far bank with a series of slack 'S' casts we induced four rises, we connected and landed one and missed the other three!

40

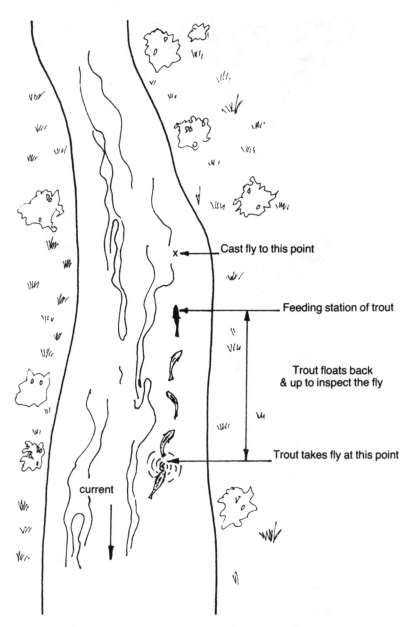

Fig. 15   The Rise

The bend in this pasture stream creates two 'Change of Pace' zones. See Appendix 'A' (2)

Dry Fly Tactics (1)

Unlike the usual slow easy rise of the chalk stream trout, our hillstream trout dart at the fly with unbelievable speed. Our strike must be almost instantaneous and at the same time quite deliberate to take up the slack 'S' curves in the line. It is inevitable that we will miss some fish. Our ratio of victories will improve with practise.

We can now move up the stream and look for other likely lies. There is a very rocky section a little further on which usually holds a few good fish. Trout like to hold position both in front of and behind rocks. In both positions the 'change of pace rule' applies as the main current separates round the rock and leaves a slack cushioned pocket of water both in front of the rock and behind. It is important whether the rock is beneath the surface or protrudes above, because trout behind a protruding rock get little chance of taking surface food. Submerged rocks can be fished over successfully with a dry fly, but a protruding rock is better left to when a wet fly is being used. See Fig.14.

Now we have reached the rocky section we can see how turbulent the water is made by the rocks. Surface turbulence signifies rocks below the surface which create turbulence downstream of their position. See Fig.14. Most dry fly fishers ignore this type of water completely, but as we mentioned – trout love it.

There is a technique that can be used on this type of water that is common practice in the USA, where it is referred to as 'fishing pocket water'. The method is just as useful in the UK. A very large dry fly is needed, almost any fly will do but it has to be large, a size 10 would not be too large. The tippet also needs to be changed to at least 2x diameter, and it can be quite short. For the kind of fishing we are about to indulge in a long leader would be a hindrance.

The idea is to flick the large dry fly onto the most turbulent areas. Just flick the fly to the surface, then as the fly is drowned in the rough water make a false cast and flick to another spot. Keep the fly moving, it only has to land on the water then it is lifted off, false cast, then flicked back to a different spot. It sounds ridiculous, but amazingly it works!

The water is never as turbulent subsurface and quite large fish hold in almost slack water on the rocky stream bed. They get very little time to study carefully any passing food and the sudden appearance of the large dry fly is very enticing – even when in a semi-drowned state. A very fast turbulent stretch of water should never be passed by – it contains fish.

It has often been said that the dry fly season does not properly start until May and that fishing a dry fly before that date is just non-productive. The following true incident will rather prove otherwise.

One day in late November I was grayling fishing on the Derbyshire Dove. The weather was exceedingly poor, the temperature was in the region of 3°C and a light snowfall was turning the landscape white. The grayling fishing was proving to be a disaster and any flyfisher in their right mind would have called it a day and gone home to a warm fireside.

On the opposite bank of the river were a number of houses with back gardens reaching down to the waterside. Several of the houses had a retaining brick wall at the end of their gardens with the wall forming the river bank.

Suddenly a definite rise was seen alongside one of the brick walls, after a short pause another rise at the same spot, shortly followed by another. Obviously a feeding fish. The light snow had intensified to a quite heavy fall and there was little prospect of fly life, insect life or terrestrials being readily available, however, the steady rises continued. The fish was obviously feeding on something.

The heavy goldhead fly that was in use was quickly taken off the tippet and substituted with a dry fly. For no reason at all a large ginger variant, size 14, was selected.

The first cast was made and the fly landed within a few inches of the wall, after a float of no more than 6in it was taken and an obviously good fish put a bend into the rod.

About five minutes later a fine 18in, (out of season), brown trout was being carefully returned to the river.

Fish are weird creatures and we must not have dogmatic ideas as to the right season for the dry fly. If the wet fly is failing to produce, then by all means prospect with a dry fly regardless of the weather. Always remember the river Dove brown that took a dry fly in the snow!

6

Fly Presentation and Drag

The problem of drag is so important that it is necessary to consider it from all aspects.

It is an old saying that 90 per cent of all fish are caught by 10 per cent of anglers. How true! What is not so loudly said is that the 10 per cent who catch the most fish are those who are constantly aware of drag. Let us try and define in detail what we are now discussing.

Drag is an unnatural movement of the artificial fly on the water surface, it may be a fast or slow movement, caused by a force on the fly exerted by the flyline or leader due to wind or water currents.

All well and good, but we must also be fully aware that the drag may be almost imperceptible to us, and only too apparent to the fish.

If an artificial fly is dropped onto the water unconnected to line and leader it will follow the natural line of the current without hinderance, in exactly the manner of a natural fly. It is when it is connected to a line and leader that are subject to differing current flows, that the problems commence.

Before we consider how we might endeavour to overcome drag remember that it is almost impossible to eliminate *all* drag. Nevertheless, we can do a great deal to reduce drag to an acceptable level. That is to say an acceptable level to the fish rather than to us!

Perhaps the easiest way to reduce drag is the most

obvious that is so often overlooked: TRY TO CAST FROM THE MOST ADVANTAGEOUS POSITION.

If we think about it we will all agree that many times we have cast to fish across varying currents and our presentation has caused almost immediate drag. With a little thought and effort we might have easily moved to a more advantageous position, perhaps only a few feet away, and made a much better job of the cast.

It is a sad fact that we so seldom pause to study the situation whenever we see a rise. Before we have considered the various currents between us and the rising fish, before we have looked for an advantageous position to cast from, we attempt to make a presentation. It is a formula for failure.

Another way to help reduce drag is to pay particular attention to the way we pick-up a fly if it has failed to tempt the fish.

Let us think about the situation that may confront us before turning our attention to the actual pick-up of the fly.

Firstly, when we see a rise, (rise-rings), on the water surface we must remember that the current has already moved the rise-rings downstream from the actual spot the natural fly was taken. Also, a rising fish moves back and up to take a fly, then returns upstream to its feeding position. See Fig.15.

Consequently, the fish that is back in the feeding position is somewhat upstream from where we first saw the rise. How far upstream is a matter of conjecture, it depends on the speed of the current and how wary the fish was of the fly that was taken. Therefore it is good dry fly fishing practice to present a fly several feet upstream from where the rise-rings were first seen.

Now we can see why the fly pick-up is so important. If

we lift-off prematurely we may be dragging the fly in the feeding zone of the fish. It may also be that the fish is drifting back prior to taking our fly. The dragging lift-off will put down any fish that is in the vicinity.

Always let the fly continue the float way past the suspected position of the feeding fish. Even when the fly is well out of the feeding zone the lift-off should be very gentle with as little disturbance as possible.

Now for what may be considered, in some quarters, pure heresy – why not consider fishing the fly *downstream* to the rising fish?

The downstream cast will only give you one chance at the fish, but if correctly executed the presentation will be almost entirely drag free.

The trick is to cast the fly downstream to a point well above the rising fish. Immediately start paying out line through the rod rings while holding the rod parallel to the water and pointing at the fish. The best way is to fast-strip line from the reel and shake the rod tip from side to side so that loose coils of line are lying on the water under the rod tip.

If there is enough slack line the fly will pass over the fish drag free. In fact the fly will enter the feeding zone ahead of the line and leader. However, if the fly is not taken the act of retrieving the fly will definitely put the fish down.

Once we fully realise how much we can reduce drag with a little care and thought we can also employ mechanical (casting) methods. The casting methods are the least effective way to reduce drag and are only used to supplement our strategic efforts.

Many fishing writers advocate using curved casts. However, how many fishing associates do you know who are masters of the curved cast? I like to think I can make a curved cast, but on reflection I must admit it only

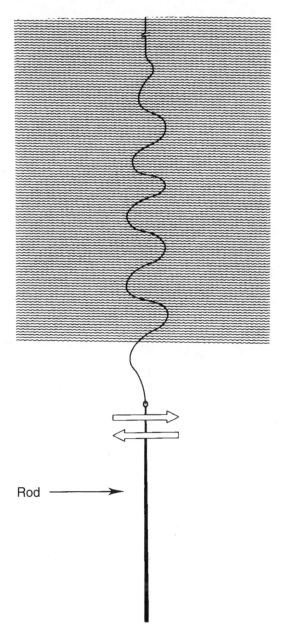

Rod ⟶

Fig. 16   The 'Lazy S' Cast

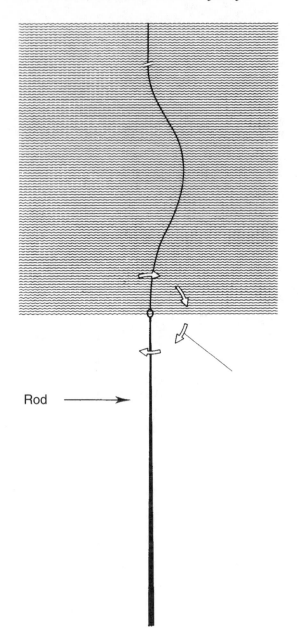

Rod ⟶

Fig. 17   The Upstream Mend

happens successfully from time to time. A 'reach cast' is possibly easier to perform, but again it is not commonly used as it basically needs personal professional instruction before it can be performed consistently well.

I think that the 'Lazy S' cast, (Fig.16) is probably the best approach to the casting problem. It is easy to understand and very easy to perform. It rarely results in a bungled cast. Sometimes the effect of the 'Lazy S' cast can even be prolonged to produce a longer drag-free float by making one or two simple line mends. See Fig.17.

Whichever way the drag problem is approached one hard and fast rule must be obeyed . . . always have slack line on the water during the critical part of the fly's float, a beautifully executed straight line cast has no place in dry fly presentation.

We must now look at another aspect of drag that is a complete paradox to all that has been written so far . . .

7

Drag and a Paradox

Over the years nearly all theories on angling have proved to be controversial. It is one of the joys of our sport that there is so much lively discussion. It is good for the sport as well as entertaining, for out of the many heated debates much knowledge has been gained.

One of the causes of so much discussion is the number of times the theories result in a complete paradox. It is one such paradox that we are concerned with here, for it applies to the subject of drag.

The caddis fly, or sedge as it is more commonly called in the UK, makes a complete mockery of all the theories on drag that we have previously discussed. However, before we proceed much further let us take a close look at this specific fly.

There are about 185 different species of caddis that belong to the order *Trichoptera*, however, many are far too small or regional in distribution to be of interest to the flyfisherman. Only a mere handful concern us, and several of these species may be on the water at the same time.

In appearance the sedge is not unlike a moth, but is usually of more slender build and carries its wings close to, and covering the body almost like a tent roof.

The adult sedge emerges from a pupae which, because of its heavily fringed legs, is a very strong swimmer. Thus the swim to the surface and the emergence is an energetic affair causing some disturbance. On emergence the adult caddis, after a very short rest, scutters along the water surface towards dry land, causing a great deal of further disturbance.

How the above facts influence our theories on drag are perhaps best illustrated by two separate incidents that happened many miles apart.

I was on a fishing holiday in the USA and visited an old friend who had a caravan, (called a trailer in the USA), on a site in a vacation park situated in the Adirondak mountain range of Upper New York State. It was a beautiful spot well kept and landscaped. My friend's trailer was situated on the bank of a man-made lake of about three acres.

Whilst sitting outside the trailer admiring the view, I spotted several rise-rings on the lake. My friend told me that he had never seen anyone fish the lake and had no idea what fish might be present but I was welcome to fish if I wanted to.

After our evening meal, as the sun went down, I put a rod together and made my way down the bank to the water. No fish were rising so I decided to try a small muddler-minnow fished slowly just below the surface.

I made the first cast and the muddler decided to float on the surface – not what I wanted at all – so I gave several sharp pulls on the line to sink the fly. The muddler proved obstinate and skittered along on the surface. Instantly the water seemed to explode around the muddler and I was fast into a fish. It was a small-mouth bass of about one pound.

After as many casts, using the same skittering technique, I had caught five more bass. It was at that point as the sun went down and dusk fell, that I was attacked by mosquitoes. Being heavily outnumbered and suffering numerous vicious bites I surrendered and withdrew to the safety of the trailer.

Before we delve into the attraction of a deliberatel
dragged fly, let us consider the second incident that wa
mentioned. This time I was much closer to home and w
were fishing a river in South Devon.

It had been a singularly unsuccessful day. Severa
splashy rises had been seen but no fish could be induce
to take any interest in our flies. Although a lot of effor
had gone into trying to discover what the fish wer
taking, we were none the wiser and had concluded tha
terrestrials were probably being blown onto the water.

In desperation I selected a particularly hairy Wulff typ
fly hoping it would act as an attractor. Time went by an
still I failed to interest any fish.

We all decided that the fish had won the day and it wa
time to pack up and head for home. I commenced to ree
in the hairy Wulff at quite a fast pace, fast enough to for
a decided wake behind it. To my utter surprise a secon
wake formed behind the fly and it was savagely take
The fish was a two pound brown, a very good fish for tha
particular South Devon river where the lively brown
were normally two to three fish to the pound.

On both the above occasions the fish (1) took a larg
hairy fly that (2) caused a commotion on the wate
surface, and (3) was dragging very badly. In other word
a fly that defied the theories of drag but was emulatin
caddis emergence behaviour. So, we must accept th
paradox that where caddis imitation is attempted ou
rules on drag do not apply.

We are left with the twin problems of fly selection ar
when to use such a technique. It has been noted on sever.
occasions that there seems little pattern to caddis eme
gence. They seem to appear at all odd times, sometim
more often than not without being noticed.

If caddis are seen to be emerging then the problem
when to use the technique is solved. Personally at oth

times I reserve the technique for use on overcast and humid days, usually after rain, when the water is a little coloured. It seems to me that caddis become active at such times and the fish are able to see the disturbance when other food is not as visible.

As to the fly to use, there are many first class imitations. Perhaps, the best known is the Welshman's Button, and Skues' Little Brown Sedge certainly takes a lot of beating.

However, as usual, I have my own preference which is none other than our old friend the Bi-Visible. See Fig.21 (page 76). We already know what a wonderful floater it is, perfect for scuttering across the water surface and giving the impression of movement. In fact, it is almost identical to a standard sedge imitation, but with the wing omitted. Experience has shown me that without doubt the fish are not at all concerned about the missing wing!

It is now time for us to go fishing again . . .

8

Dry Fly Tactics (2)

Our next fishing session together will be during late June and on a limestone river. We are going to fish a river in the Peak District that takes the majority of its water from the limestone hills via countless springs, some of which originate in the limestone caves of the area.

The spring water has sometimes taken years to permeate through the limestone terrain becoming decidedly alkaline in the process, (ph 7.6 to 8.4). The rainfall of years back reappears in the form of crystal clear alkaline spring water. Many areas in the Dales bottle such water commercially, it has the reputation of being some of the purest water in the UK.

Although our river is a very close relative to a chalk stream it does not conform to the lowland pasture/water meadow format that is a general feature of our southern chalk streams. Our river is on the wild side as it flows through the craggy terrain of the Dales. We have many features before us that are not commonly seen on southern chalk streams. We have numerous weirs resulting in sparkling miniature waterfalls, there are also very deep mysterious pools of limpid green-tinged water connected by stretches of fast rippling shallows. Some of the banks are reasonably clear but others are densely wooded.

The alkaline water, as in the chalk streams, promotes prolific underwater plant life that harbours a multitude of life forms – nymphs, crustaceans, larvae and water beetles etc. – all of which are food for the trout. The lime-stone river trout lives a much more comfortable lifestyle than his hillstream relative. The fairly constant water level and flow, plus the prolific food supply result in larger, stronger and well formed fish. The limestone river trout can afford to be choosy about his food, he can feed leisurely and selectively on the variety available.

The average size trout we can expect today is probably between ¾lb and 1½lb, with every hope of perhaps a 2lb fish.

Before we start fishing let us think about the general problems that will confront us.

Although flylife is quite prolific on this river, hatches are inclined to be spasmodic and of very short duration. Quite often we will see numerous flies over the water only to realise that they are spinners that have resulted from a previous hatch that we did not see. As on the hillstream we would be in for rather a futile day if we just waited for a general rise to a hatch. We will certainly see more rises here than on the hillstream, mostly to spent spinners on the water, dead or dying after egg laying. Some of the rises seen will be to terrestrials and during this period of mid-summer terrestrials form about 30 per cent of the trout's daily diet.

At this time of year the mayfly season is over, (this river has very good mayfly hatches), and the fish have been feeding well. Now is the time for evening hatches of pale wateries, and often sedge hatches are also part of the evening programme. During the day a few medium olives may come off the water for very short periods, and if the day is particularly cold and windy we might see a few iron blues.

Of course, we will keep our eyes open to spot any rises that indicate the location of a fish, but for most of the time we will be prospecting likely lies. If we are going to match the medium olive spinners that the fish might expect to see then we should use a Lunn's Particular fly. However, it has been found many times that a Grey Duster with the bottom half of the hackle trimmed away is a real fish catcher on the limestone rivers when medium olive spent spinners are on the water. Use what you think is best, but the Grey Duster trick is a good tip from my experience.

Our golden 'change of pace rule' will always apply regardless of the type of water. Here on a limestone river the rule has wider implications. Many features of the river create a 'change of pace' without it being immediately apparent.

The weirs send fast water over their edge, but immediately in front of the face of the weir is a back-wash type of eddy. The back-wash area is very small but nevertheless a 'change of pace' is created. We will also see several small islands along the river. Where the current divides in front of and behind the island a slack cushion of water is formed, in this way another 'change of pace' is created. Weedbeds are prolific and we will see that the current divides into numerous channels between the weedbeds. Under the weedbeds many stems go down to anchor in the river bed, they break up the main current flow and form another 'change of pace' area.

It is time we started fishing . . .

We can make our way upstream and cast our trimmed Grey Duster onto the channels between the weedbeds. It is best to first fish the channels that are closest to us. The old problem of drag is back with us, and back with a vengeance! To reach the clear channels we have to cast over weedbeds and the caught-up line causes immediate drag. It is a frustrating experience, we know the fish are in the 'change of pace' zone under the weedbeds, but we also know they will not take a dragging fly.

Dry Fly Tactics (2)

The answer to the problem lies in a change to our tackle set-up. If we lengthen our tippet by another 3ft we will have a 9ft leader plus 6ft of tippet, overall a 15ft leader. We can now consider that if we extend only 2yd of flyline beyond the rod tip, we can present a fly up to approximately 30ft away – i.e. length of rod plus 2yd of line plus 15ft of leader. Total approximately 30ft and *all with only 2yd of flyline in use*!

With only, for the main part, tippet material caught up over the weedbeds it is surprising how little drag is created. We will not obtain long drag-free floats, but short floats between the weedbeds are all we require.

When we take a fish we will be confronted with a further problem, how to get it out of the weedbed! There is really no answer to this problem you just fall back on experience and do the best you can. You win some, and you lose some. It's the same for all of us.

When we come to the numerous weirs we will be confronted with the necessity of a different kind of presentation. Working our way upstream and casting upstream brings us to the face of a weir with the water cascading over towards us. If we cast to the face of the weir the fly will land in the fast water and be carried speedily towards us in a semi-drowned condition. That is not the result we wish to achieve.

Provided we make no sudden movements or cause underwater disturbance we can approach a weir either by wading, or walking along the bank, much closer than we would normally approach a trout lie. The cascading water plus the surface turbulence hides our presence from the fish. We can take advantage of this fact and gain a position that will enable us to make a short cast to the water that is above the weir. The fly will be carried over the weir and be trapped momentarily in the back-wash eddy just where we want it.

The Small Stream Dry Fly

Some time back I was carrying out this manoeuvre when the fly was taken whilst it was on the water above the weir. The fish decided to play out the game in the pool above and a mad scramble resulted as I attempted to climb out of the water to get above the weir as quickly as possible. The incident is worth remembering, it could happen again.

It is also worth remembering that a weir is normally at the tail of a reasonable pool, and that the tail of a pool is a favourite feeding station for trout. If the tail of a pool is rocky and provides cover it is always a 'change of pace' area worth fishing over. However, the immediate area above a weir, although a 'change of pace' area, normally offers little cover and trout are usually wary of it during daylight hours.

As we progress upstream it is common to find rustic footbridges over many limestone streams that run through the Dales. Bridges provide wonderful cover for trout and although not truly a 'change of pace' area, the advantages of deeper water and protective cover outweigh the disadvantages.

Whilst we are considering bridges, a further important incident comes to mind that also illustrates a point to be remembered.

One day as I walked across a footbridge on this very limestone stream, a trout of about 10in to 12in was seen lying under the bridge. The terrain and layout of the river made an upstream cast under the bridge impossible, so it was decided to go above the bridge and make a downstream cast with a very slack line so as to avoid drag.

The terrain above the bridge was also a problem. Wading out into the stream was possible but the banks were densely wooded and foliage overhanging the stream made casting extremely difficult. To add to the problems there was only a gap of about 4ft under the bridge. A side cast made no more than 1ft above the water was the only way to put a fly successfully under the bridge.

A couple of false casts were made to extend line, and on making the final forward cast a solid resistance on the extended back cast was felt. Instead of being caught-up in the overhanging foliage, as at first suspected, a trout had taken the fly as it had possibly lightly touched the water on the backcast. The fish was the best ever taken by me from this particular stream, a 2¼lb brown in fine condition. This incident shows how briefly a dry fly needs to be on the water without drag to attract a fish.

It is now clear why fishing between weedbeds with free floats of only a few inches can be so successful. It also explains the success of briefly flicking a fly from place to place over turbulent water. Long floats are not necessary, drag-free floats are the complete answer.

9

Dry Fly Tactics (3)

The Lowland/Pasture Water

The lowland or pasture water is most often one or other of two types. It may be a naturally slow flowing lowland water, generally with a muddy river bed, that during its entire water course has never been a hillstream. Such water usually has a predominance of coarse fish but the odd trout may be encountered. These trout are usually older and larger fish, often cannibal, that have dropped downstream from the upper reaches for easier living conditions.

The other type of lowland water is the hillstream or limestone river that whilst pursuing its water course has left its hilly or mountainous origins behind and is now flowing through the floor of a valley or reasonably flat farmland. It is on this second type of water that we are now going to fish together during the latter part of the season.

Our river is a limestone stream that has left the limestone hills far behind, it is miles from its source and is presently flowing through cultivated farmland. The banks are now quite high as the river is subject to flooding from rain water running off the surrounding land. The water is no longer quite so alkaline for it has picked up acid elements from the surrounding terrain, but it is a long way from becoming a predominantly acid stream.

Dry Fly Tactics (3)

The stream bed is still mainly gravel, and rocks are plentiful, but some of the slower flowing sections have somewhat silted up. Underwater plant life thrives, but not to the same extent as found in the higher reaches.

The food supply for the trout is plentiful and, in fact, is even more profuse than higher upstream. The normal food supply is supplemented by many terrestrials off the surrounding rich farmland soil. Also the silty fine gravel sections of riverbed give rise to large quantities of 'black fly', (mostly *Simulium* species).

As we fish this stretch of river we must vary some of the tactics we used when fishing the upper reaches in the area of the Dales. The weedbeds are not so prolific but we still need to fish the channels between them using our over-length leader. We must also look carefully for other 'change of pace' areas, although in this sector they are not so easy to find.

One 'change of pace' area that we can easily locate is where there is a curve or bend in the river. It may not be readily apparent but the outside curve of the bend, close to the bank, is a first-class 'change of pace' area. A series of drag-free floats along such a bank with an appropriate fly will often result in a solid rise. If the bank is wooded a terrestrial offering could be even more appropriate and tempting.

It was while fishing at a similar location that I decided to float a black deerhair beetle imitation downstream very close to the curved bank. This was accomplished by making a short cast then stripping line off the reel and paying it out by shaking it through the rod-rings. A long float was necessary and a lot of line had been paid out before the deerhair beetle was solidly taken with a rise from a very good trout.

Generally speaking the water current through this area of farmland is slower, and the water deeper, than found higher upstream. We must always remember that the trout have much more time to look carefully over our offerings and the very close scrutiny of our flies is not in our favour. We must be very careful with our fly selection, and be careful to avoid as much drag as possible on our flies. It is perhaps true to say that the flies used here should be a size or two smaller than usual if they are to be really effective. The smaller the fly the less detail is visible during close scrutiny. If any fly that we use induces a rise but is not taken, it is a good indication that something smaller is needed.

It is often surprising that after we have been fishing this sector for some time with varying success the water is suddenly covered with small dimple rises. At the same time no fly hatch can be discerned. The most probable reason is a hatch of *Simulium reptans*, a small black fly that is often mistaken for the *Bibio johannis* that most anglers call Black Gnats. The *Bibio johannis* is actually a terrestrial so the dimple rises seen are most likely to the aquatic *Simulium*. It can become a frustrating experience as it is extremely difficult to take advantage of such a hatch, small all-black dry flies are often too large and are not attractive to the fish.

We should bear in mind that *Simulium reptans* pupate under water and the fly rises to the surface in a bubble of air that appears to the fish as a tiny shining silver globe. If we use a very small – size 20/22 is ideal – black hackled fly that has a silver tinsel body, the results are often quite gratifying. The fly needs to be on a very fine tippet, 6x or 7x, and to be completely free of floatant. Our objective is to cast among the numerous rises a fly that sinks down into and under the surface film.

In practice it is not difficult to obtain a rise to our fly, the problem is to recognise the rise amongst all the others that are around it. It sometimes helps to put a very tiny coloured indicator about 12in along the tippet from our fly. It at least indicates the approximate position of our fly among the many rises.

Not all of this stretch of river is deep and slow flowing. There are several rock formations and rock shelving that create shallow riffles for short distances. Trout are apt to congregate at the tail of these faster flows and our 'change of pace rule' will enable us to locate these lies.

The choice of fly is difficult. It is clear to us that any dead or dying spinners would be well drowned and be subsurface before they reached the trout lies at the tail of the riffles. If the fish are to be induced to rise we need to think along the lines of hatching duns. It is under these conditions that the various 'emerger' patterns are so effective. Possibly any good emerger pattern might bring results but a hot favourite must be the 'Klinkhamer' type, mainly because they are so easily seen on the fast rippling water. However, we must again stress the need for smaller fly sizes on these lowland waters. The usual large Klinkhamer, (normally size 12) must be scaled down to at least size 16. See Fig.18. The wing colour of these smaller Klinkhamers seems to be irrelevant to the trout, consequently a wing colour that is easily seen by us should be chosen. Pink or yellow are both a very good choice.

Whilst fishing our lowland water it is only too easy to forget how the high banks can easily ruin our results. We are inclined to ignore how clearly we are seen by the fish when we walk along the top of these high banks. Very often we are not only seen but are also a stark silhouette against the skyline. Some of the banks are 6ft or more above the water level, evidence of how severe the flood water can be when it drains directly off the surrounding terrain.

It is often quite difficult to get off the skyline by wading the stream due to the mud and silt composition of the

The Small Stream Dry Fly

streambed. The water of this stream is seldom too deep for wading, but wading on a very soft muddy streambed, even in fairly shallow water, can be quite hazardous. Nevertheless we must try to wade whenever we can so that our profile is kept low to the water. A wading staff is a terrific asset under these circumstances.

We do not require the robust heavy wading staff of the angler who fishes whilst wading chest high in strong water. We only require a lightweight short staff that can steady us over a rocky streambed and also be used to probe for deep mud before we get into difficulties.

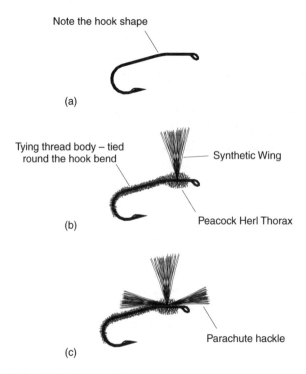

Fig. 18   The Klinkhamer Fly

66

Many years ago I invested in a lightweight elasticated folding staff that fits snugly into a holster on my belt. Once withdrawn from the holster it 'springs into action'. Not a cheap item, but it has been invaluable through the years.

It would be appropriate here to give a final word of warning. This lowland water can, as evidenced by the high banks, have the water level raised enormously as a result of a heavy rainstorm. Sometimes the rainfall is not even local but a fair way upstream. Also the water level does not always rise slowly, it depends on the severity of the storm and we can be caught unawares when wading in very rapidly rising water. At the first sign of this happening leave the water immediately. The lower reaches of a hillstream are no place to be wading when the water is rising rapidly.

10

Dry Fly Tactics (4)

The Moorland Stream

Most of us, when we hear the words 'moorland stream', conjure up a certain mental picture. We think of a craggy, possibly hilly, expanse of barren land, windswept and bleak, with rock and boulder strewn streams tumbling through it.

The mental picture is only partially true. I have many times fished streams that fall into the above category, and delightful streams they are, but only a few moorland waters are of this type.

The moorlands of the West of England and those in the Northern Counties, are vast areas with landscapes so diverse that many types of river and stream may be found.

It is true to say that, with a couple of exceptions, the waters in moorland areas are not chalk or limestone streams. However, the point being made is that the stereotype moorland stream is not the only type of water that will be encountered.

One thing most of the rivers and streams have in common is that they are rain-fed off the surrounding terrain, are subject to sudden rises in water volume, and are slightly acid. Most are also tinged with that lovely whisky shade that comes from a boggy or peaty terrain.

To fish these rivers and streams you have to put into practice the arts and techniques learned on waters elsewhere. At times you will fish using the tactics of the hillstream, including the specialised skill of fishing 'pocket water' with an oversized fly. At other times the tactics will be those used on lowland waters, especially in the vicinity of moorland towns or villages that are usually located on the fringes of the moor.

The small turbulent moorland streams that are near their source very often change their character radically as they reach the perimeters of the moor. They become rivers in their own right, some even major rivers as they approach a coastline.

The small 6in to 8in brown/golden highly coloured trout of the tiny upland moorland stream becomes in the lower reaches the brown of several pounds weight.

I am reminded of the largest brown trout I have ever seen from a moorland stream. I was staying at a hotel located in a town on the fringe of Dartmoor. The hotel was built on the banks of a well known river and the dining room windows looked out onto a lovely bridge-pool. I was having my dinner one evening while sitting at a window table when just a few yards away a large trout began to rise regularly in the pool. The trout was clearly in view and although it was difficult to judge accurately its weight a fair guess would be in the region of 3lb to 4lb. Don't believe anyone who tells you all moorland trout are small!

I suppose that the vast open area of the moors has something to do with it, the weather certainly becomes a major problem for moorland anglers. It seems to me that almost every time I have fished on either Dartmoor, Exmoor or Bodmin moor it has been in a high wind and lashing rain. Rivers and streams are apt to rise at an alarming rate. On one occasion I was fishing at Mary Tavy on Dartmoor and the river changed to a roaring torrent during the short time I was fishing. It was quite a dangerous situation. Great care must be taken on the moors and the environment treated with the utmost respect.

It was mentioned above that the rock pools, (pocket water), that are found on moorland head-waters could be fished in the same manner as similar water on the hill-streams. (See Chapter 5.) However, there are some differences.

The rock pools on the moorland stream are usually much smaller and shallower than we have encountered previously. The stream is sometimes only a few feet wide and the rocks now become the size of boulders. Also, due to the open nature of the terrain we are so easily seen by the trout inhabiting the small shallow pools. Because the trout are small does not mean they are young and immature, they are often adult experienced fish.

If you are to be successful you must take advantage of every little bit of available cover. If cover is scarce then keep well back from the bank, keep low by kneeling, and extend the cast further than usual.

The use of the over-sized dry fly on these headwater rock pools is still a good tactic, but for the little fellows in these small pools a size 14 fly is quite large enough. The use of a size 10 Bi-Visible would probably scatter them in all directions.

When the small streams reach the fringes of the moor they can often be fished as a 'lowland water'. Terrestrials that were almost useless upstream can now be tried. The usual problem is the colour in the water that seems to intensify the further downstream you travel. Also the streambed is more often muddy than clean. However, it is in the lower reaches that the largest trout will be found.

The moors can be desolate places and the weather often atrocious, but they are never over-crowded, and solitude is sometimes a valuable commodity.

11

Specialist Flies

During our previous fishing forays to rivers and streams of various types we discussed dry fly tactics for different conditions and situations. Several of those situations and the methods of fishing them could, at times, prove quite difficult with the standard dry flies from our suggested restricted flybox.

An additional four types of specialist flies added to our flybox could usefully improve our armoury. They are: the mini-Klinkhamer, reverse-tied standard flies, half-hackle standard flies and bi-visibles.

At this juncture I would like to make one point absolutely clear. Although various flies have been recommended for our small stream flybox, to which the additional specialist flies mentioned above can be added, only suggestions are being made. The contents of flyboxes are an individual and personal thing. We all have favourite flies that we have faith in and other flies we dislike using. In most cases it is because we have no faith in the flies we dislike that we fish them in a dilatory fashion, consequently results are usually poor.

Choose your own flybox contents, the suggestions made in these pages are intended as general help only. Now let us discuss specialist flies . . .

The Mini-Klinkhamer

In Chapter 9, mention was made of the mini-Klinkhamer and its usefulness in special circumstances.

The Klinkhamer fly was designed by Hans van Klinken, (a Dutch flyfisher), primarily for grayling fishing on European waters. Although the originator specified in detail the correct materials for the pattern, it was very quickly apparent that the fly was not so much a specific fly as a concept that lent itself to a large variety of patterns, tied in all sizes with all manner of materials. For interest, the original pattern is tied as follows:

Original Klinkhamer

Hook: Size 12 specially bent (similar to a sedge hook).

Thread: Black

Body: Hare's-ear, tied very sparse and round the bend of the hook

Thorax: Peacock herl, round base of wing

Wing: White synthetic yarn

Hackle: Blue dun, tied parachute style round base of wing

If you study a Klinkhamer fly for a few moments it becomes very clear that the design is intended to represent a hatching aquatic fly, commonly called an emerger. The body of the fly is intended to hang down below the water surface supported by the thorax and the parachute hackle that represents legs. The pronounced thorax is intended to simulate the emerging fly. Trout do not seem to relate to the wing which becomes purely a sighting aid for the angler. There is no doubt whatever, the design is a stroke of genius.

Whilst we were fishing together in Chapter 9, we talked about using a 'mini' Klinkhamer. The following is a pattern which may prove useful:

Mini-Klinkhamer. See Fig.18.

Hook: 16 or 18 long-shank bent to shape shown

Thread: Colour intended for body

Body: Tying thread kept thin and tied well round hook bend

Thorax: Hare's-ear dubbing – a pinch round base of wing

Wing: Synthetic yarn – yellow or pink (sometimes fluorescent)

Hackle   Grizzle, tied parachute round base of wing

The Reversed-Tied Fly

The long leader tactics we employed in Chapter 8, when we fished our flies on the channels between the weedbeds, can be helped by the use of a reversed-tied fly.

Again, this is not a fly pattern, although the idea probably became popular with a fly called the Leckford Professor which was devised by Ernest Mott, a chalk stream river keeper. A look at Fig.19 will show that it is a design that can be applied to almost any standard dry fly.

Tying the hackle at the bend of the hook rather than at the eye has the advantage of semi-hiding and guarding the hook point. It appears to make absolutely no difference to the trout, and although some writers maintain that hooking properties are impaired no such problems have ever been encountered.

Fig. 19   The Reverse-Hackle Fly

The advantage of the reverse-hackle fly is that it is less likely to get caught up in floating weed as the hook point is lightly guarded. It is inevitable that at the end of many a good float through a weed channel the standard dry fly snags itself before it can be lifted off the water. A reverse-hackle fly almost does away with the problem.

At the first attempt the fly may prove difficult to tie and the following hints will be of help:

1. Tie the hackle first, not the body.

2. Tie the hackle on the shank of the hook – do not go round the bend (!).

3. Start tying the body at the hackle and end at the eye.

4. A tail is not necessary – the tippet acts as the tail.

The Half-Hackle Fly

Several times whilst we were fishing together we mentioned that the fish were, in all probability, taking spinners.

The sequence of the emergence of the aquatic fly is for the nymph to first hatch as a dun, then to moult to a spinner. The emerging nymph only becomes a floating dun for a short period of time during which the hatched dun dries its wings prior to flying off the water. The trout love to feed on the floating duns, but they are not so easy to secure as the later moulted spinners. That is the reason why the trout, during a hatch, often seem to take crippled duns in preference to the fully hatched insects. Crippled duns can't get away!

After moulting to spinners the flies mate and the female lays her eggs. Some varieties of female spinners fly low over the water and drop their eggs, others enter the water and lay their eggs subsurface.

The end result is always the same, after mating and egg laying many male and female spinners lie dying or dead on the water surface. At this stage they are a very easy target for hungry trout.

For some years I have not bothered to tie specific spinner patterns for use on small streams, quite simply because I have not found it necessary to do so. There is always the problem of knowing which variety of spent

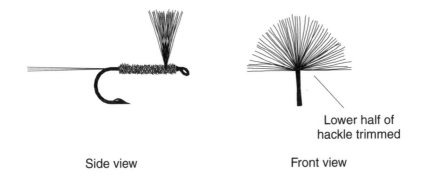

Lower half of
hackle trimmed

Side view   Front view

Fig. 20   The Trimmed Grey Duster

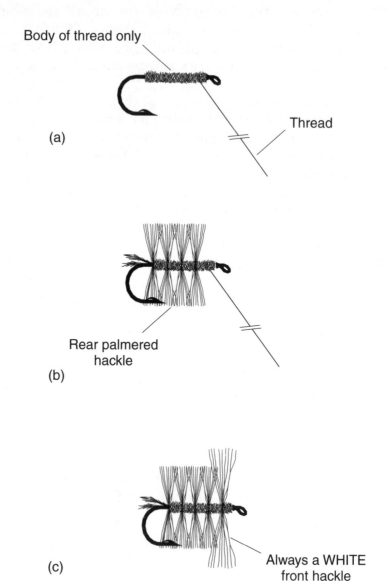

Body of thread only

Thread

(a)

Rear palmered
hackle

(b)

Always a WHITE
front hackle

(c)

Fig. 21   The Bi-Visible Fly

spinners the fish are taking. It might not be a problem on a chalk stream after a prolific hatch but on our type of stream where the hatches are infrequent and not always seen, it is a very different matter.

My method of overcoming the difficulty is to trim off the lower half of the hackle on a Grey Duster. See Fig.20. The fly then sits low with its body in the surface film, the sides of the hackle rest on the water imitating spent wings. The trout seem to ignore the upper half of the hackle, but it does enable us to see the fly more clearly.

I have found this little ploy quite successful and have no hesitation in recommending it.

The Bi-Visible

When we fished the rock pools, (pocket water), together in Chapter 5 the use of a larger than usual dry fly was suggested. The fly employed not only needs to be large but it must also be as buoyant as possible. The problem with the majority of large dry flies is that they tend to be bulky as well as large and also very poor imitations of natural insects.

The search for a dry fly that can be tied in a large size, have very little bulk, is a first class floater, and can also be clearly seen by the angler when used on turbulent water, leads us to the Bi-Visible.

The Bi-Visible is not a new fly, Ray Bergman reported its use on USA waters in *Trout* (published by Alfred A. Knopf, New York, way back in the 1930s). The origins are not known but the design leads us to believe that it was one of the ancient wet flies that successfully became a dry fly.

Once again there is no pattern, just a design that can be modified with various materials to suit the occasion.

The Bi-Visible. See Fig.21

Hook:	8 to 16 long shank
Thread:	Colour as body hackle
Tail:	Two hackle points, same as body hackle
Body:	Tying thread
Body Hackle:	Tied palmer – colour as required
Front Hackle:	Always white

Basically speaking the Bi-Visible has no body. The tying thread covers the hook shank in the usual touching turns as a seating for the body hackle which is tied 'palmer'. Sufficient space is left at the head of the fly for the white hackle. Someone once described the Bi-Visible as a 'two-tone Flu-brush', quite an accurate description.

The finished fly is large, very light and will float and float. Time has proved its worth, trout take it with very little hesitation. It obviously gives a hazy impression of a buzzing fly lightly touching the water surface, probably a sedge.

It is certainly worthwhile to add a few Bi-Visible flies to your flybox, I suggest size 10 or 12 with body colours of brown or black. The front hackle is always white.

12

Dry Fly Tactics (5)

Fishing Micro Dry Flies

Fishing with micro dry flies, that is to say flies that are size 20, 22, 24, and perhaps even 26, is not to everyone's fancy. We are discussing them here because they exist, because they are often recommended in articles in the angling press, and because they undoubtedly catch fish.

Another reason for discussing them in these pages is that special techniques are necessary if they are to be used effectively. Also, as they are not readily available from the tackle houses most 'micros' are home tied and a few tying tips would not go amiss.

Very often it is suggested that micro flies are needed because the trout are selectively feeding on minute natural flies, and black gnats are sometimes quoted. However, a general rise to black gnats (*Simulium* species), requires a special technique as described in Chapter 9 (Dry Fly Tactics (3)), other general rises to minute naturals are rather more rare and difficult to deal with.

The main benefits we obtain from using micro patterns are two fold. (1) The fly is so small that fine detail is not so apparent to the trout and a simplified pattern is quite effective, and (2) because of the smallness of the fly we are forced to fish with more finesse using finer tippets etc., and as a result our approach is often more successful.

79

If the decision is taken to use micro flies we must choose our patterns with care and be prepared to vary our usual techniques.

The first variation that confronts us is the necessary change to our tippet material. We can use the rule devised by Darrel Martin (see *Micro Flies* published by Swan Hill Press). We divide the fly size by four to give us the 'X' rating of tippet required to pass through the eye of the fly, and at the same time be rigid enough to deliver the fly and fine enough to obtain a good natural drag-free float.

i.e.   Fly size 20 ÷ 4 = 5x

Fly size 22 ÷ 4 = 5½x

Fly size 24 ÷ 4 = 6x

Fly size 26 ÷ 4 = 6½x

An indication of the specification that could be expected of good quality nylon monofilament is as follows:

5x   = .006in dia. and 2½lb breaking strain

5½x = .0055in dia. and 2¼lb breaking strain

6x   = .005in dia. and 2lb breaking strain

6½x = .0045in dia. and 1¼lb breaking strain

Always remember that the breaking strain of nylon is drastically reduced by any knots that are tied in it.

Although it is usual practice to keep the rod well up when playing a fish a different approach is necessary when using 6x and 7x nylon.

It was Vincent Marinaro in his book *A Modern Dry Fly Code*, (Crown Publishers Inc., New York), who carried out endless experiments with fine tippets, (albeit cat-gut), some of which registered only ¼lb breaking strain.

Marinaro found that the extra friction generated by the rod-rings when the rod was held high reduced the breaking strain considerably. The best results were obtained when the rod was held low with the tip pointing at the fish.

Although Marinaro was only concerned with cat-gut, (nylon had yet to make its debut), his experimental results apply equally to the nylon of today. We are all inclined to take nylon breaking strains as stated by the manufacturers for granted. Once the tippet is knotted onto the leader, then at the fly, the breaking strain is probably halved.

Of course, we can today use the so called 'double strength' nylons. At first sight this seems to be the perfect solution. However, such nylons are usually stiffer and a little more brittle than standard grades and tend to impair the natural free float of a micro fly. It has also been noted that some anglers seem to have difficulty tying secure knots in 'double strength' nylon. Nevertheless, with care when tying knots the 'double strength' material can be very useful and give a comfortable feeling of safety. Choose the brand carefully, and buy as limp a product as you can.

Using 5x, 6x and 7x nylon creates a further problem. Few of us have the visual acuity to pass the almost invisible nylon easily through the minute eye of the fly. There are some hooks on the market labelled 'Big-Eye', whose eye is supposed to be the same size as the next largest hook. However, such hooks are very difficult to obtain in sizes 20 to 26, and it is of little help if a size 24 hook has an eye the same as a hook size 22!

I found my own solution to the problem was to purchase a watch-maker's eye glass with 4x magnification. A hole was easily made with a bradawl in the soft plastic side which enabled me to attatch a cord that could be pinned to my fishing vest. It is thus readily available whenever I want to change a micro fly and is prevented from ending up in the river.

When actually fishing a micro fly it is often almost impossible to see the fly on the water surface. This is especially true when the light is at a bad angle to the surface ripples. Of course you easily see a rise to the fly, but you must be looking at the right place which is not always easy.

It is a fact that the leader length, including tippet, always appears to the angler to be shorter than it really is. The viewing angle fore-shortens the view seen. If we place a tiny indicator onto the tippet, about 18in above the fly, it will appear to the angler to be almost where the fly is located. Such an indicator can be made with a very tiny pinch of fluorescent orange 'Float-Do', which can be obtained from most tackle outlets. The 'Float-Do' is a form of floating putty, quite easy to mould to shape, but hardens in the cold water and adheres strongly to the tippet material.

Patterns for micro flies, like standard flies are legion. Most of the many patterns will catch fish at one time or another, but a wise angler will curtail his collection to a reasonable number.

We have already suggested a solution in Chapter 9, to the *Simulium* problem. We now need a couple of patterns that will solve the problem of rises to minute terrestrials (such as small ants or beetles) and also general midges.

We would suggest that the Griffith's Gnat and the RFC Hackle Fly are eminently suitable for our purpose and at the same time are very simple to tie in the micro sizes.

The patterns are as follows:

Dry Fly Tactics (5)

Griffith's Gnat

Hook: Size 20 to 26 long shank

Silk: Black

Body: Peacock herl

Hackle: Grizzle, tied palmer

Tail: None

There are a couple of variations of the above fly that are worth consideration. Sometimes a brown or black hackle is used, but they do make the fly more difficult to see on the water.

I have my own variation that I find works for me – I trim off the bottom half of the palmered grizzle hackle so that the fly rests in the surface film of the water. I like to think that the remaining side hackle fibres represent legs.

The RFC Hackle Fly

Hook: Size 20 to 26

Silk: Black

Hackle: Silver badger

Tail   None

This fly requires a little explanation. It is a fly tied using nothing but the tying silk and a single hackle feather.

The method is to tie in a single hackle feather at the bend of the hook then to palmer the feather in *very close turns* up to the hook eye and tie-off in the usual manner. You now have a fly that looks like a minute flue-brush!

The next step is to give the fly a 'haircut' – all the hackle fibres are close trimmed from the rear half of the hook shank leaving a complete front hackle in place. The lower half of this front hackle is then trimmed off, in the same manner that we trimmed our Grey Duster in Chapter 11, (see Fig.20).

Hey presto, a one hackle fly! These flies are so easy to tie and so effective that you may be tempted to tie all your flies in this manner.

Whether or not to fish micro flies is a personal decision. If you are the type of flyfisher who enjoys fishing ultra-fine and can thrill to the capture of a good size trout on an almost invisible fly, then give it a try. It could be *you* that ends up being hooked!

13

Dry Fly Tactics (6)

Fishing Terrestrials

There is no doubt whatever that a large proportion of a
trout's diet in mid-summer is made up of terrestrial
insects.

Many scientific surveys have been carried out and obviously data varies from one location to another, but
consolidated results show that feeding on terrestrial
insects must be a major consideration.

All manner of terrestrials are taken, winged terrestrial
insects of course, but there are many others such as
grasshoppers, leaf hoppers, caterpillars, beetles, ants,
and various grubs.

All water is bounded by land and it is inevitable that
terrestrials will, mainly by accident, find themselves in or
on the water. Sometimes they jump the wrong way, at
other times they drop off foliage or are blown by the wind.
All are food for trout.

Terrestrial feeding is opportunistic feeding and cannot
be planned for. True, at times there is a virtual plague of
a particular insect, very often ants or beetles fall into this
category, but generally speaking trout cannot be selective. A tit-bit falls onto the water – there is a swirl and it
is gone!

Terrestrial Patterns

We have already discussed in Chapter 4 the desirability of having terrestrial patterns in the flybox, and have seen several recommended patterns in Figs. 10, 11 and 12.

Although commercial flytying companies are now offering better selections than in past years, their lists still leave a great deal to be desired. At one time their lists were so inadequate that all they listed were 'beetle', 'ant', 'moth' etc., it is little wonder that many anglers never bothered with terrestrials.

Since those early years a lot of work has been done to promote terrestrial fishing. Vincent Marinaro laid solid foundations in *A Modern Dry Fly Code* (Crown Publishers Inc., New York), and I hope that I personally added to the work in my book *Trout and Terrestrials*, (Swan Hill Press).

Today it is appreciated that although a terrestrial is usually taken by a trout on a 'one-off' basis, the artificial offered must truly represent a natural insect. Poor imitations do not always trigger the required reaction from trout.

Presentation

At the outset it must be appreciated that terrestrial patterns, by their very nature, are usually heavier and more bulky than standard fly patterns. It follows that certain changes have to be made to our leader set-up if a good presentation is to be achieved.

Most terrestrial patterns are within our usual hook sizes, i.e. 14, 16 and 18, (see Chapter 4), but due to weight and bulk are better presented on 3x tippets, (.008in dia. nylon). A shorter leader is also helpful to achieve a good turnover in the cast.

The secret of a good presentation is to imitate the way the particular natural insect might find itself on the water. If possible copy those circumstances and choose the likely location where it might occur.

For example, a leaf hopper or a caterpillar could fall from overhanging foliage and hit the water with a little 'plop'. A beetle might have fallen off a bank and be washed along in the current close to that bank. Grasshoppers jump in the direction they are currently facing and quite often jump off a grassy bank straight onto the water.

Trout love grasshoppers, especially the smaller young ones who paddle about vigorously when on the water surface. Our problem is the difficulty in replicating their actions. I have found small imitations, used on rough water to hide the lack of activity, will sometimes bring a strike.

Many more ants find their way into the stream than we imagine. They are almost impossible to see on the water and the rises to them are often quite baffling as to what is being taken. The example in Fig.11 (page 34) is a good pattern to use, and can be even further improved by trimming the hackle both top and bottom so that only the side barbs of the hackle remain. The ant then sinks into the water surface film supported by the side hackle. The result is a very lifelike presentation.

An example of what happened to me on one occasion will illustrate the worth of a terrestrial imitation. I had finished fishing for the day and was making my way back to the car park along a streamside path. The path was very narrow and much overgrown, on one side was the stream and on the other an almost vertical wooded hillside. Casting from the path was an absolute impossibility.

As I passed a tree whose branches were trailing into the water, I heard, rather than saw, a fish rise among the trailing branches. I stopped to watch and listen. This time I saw the fish rise, it was a good size fish and the rise was a slashing swirl.

I decided to walk on to where I could cross the stream, then to make my way back to attempt a cast from the opposite bank.

A few minutes later I was in position and surveying the problem. I would be able to cast to the trailing branches but no free float was possible before the fly would be snagged in the branches.

I decided that my presentation would have to be taken as soon as the fly touched the water, and only a terrestrial imitation landing with a 'plop' might induce such a fast strike.

A tubby little black beetle was chosen and a carefully measured cast was made to the very edge of the trailing branches. The cast was delivered with a hard downward forward stroke so that the beetle made a solid landing.

The result was immediate – a large swirl and the beetle was gone. The prize was a 1¾lb wild brown.

The lesson to be learned is that no standard fly could have been presented in a like manner. Only a terrestrial could induce such a response.

The Angler's View

Many anglers have become frustrated with terrestrial imitations and have abandoned their use because of the difficulty of seeing them on the water.

It is a fact of life that many terrestrials such as beetles, hawthorn flies, black gnats (*B. johannis*), ants etc., are all black or some other dark colour. All very difficult to see.

There are one or two 'tricks of the trade' that can be used to overcome the situation.

Very often a grizzle hackle can be used on beetles, ants

and hawthorns to a very good effect. Not only is it easier to see but it also simulates the insect's wings more realistically.

It is also possible to paint a white spot on the backs of beetles and to paint the head of an ant white. The white spots and heads do not seem to bother the fish, many fish have been taken with terrestrial lures treated in this manner.

Locating Terrestrial-Feeding Trout

In the course of these pages we have many times mentioned the 'change of pace' rule, and it must always apply to locating feeding trout. However, when we were considering the use of terrestrial imitations there are further aspects to be taken into account.

Any natural terrestrials on the water will, of course, be carried downstream by the current, and trout on feeding station will take them. The feeding station being in a 'change of pace' zone.

In addition to the regular 'change of pace' zones there are others less obvious where natural terrestrials are more abundant. Notably these are where the water is close to terrain where terrestrials abound, such as long grass, earthern banks, over-hanging trees and bushes, dense undergrowth along the bank etc. If such water can also be classed as a 'change of pace' area, then prospecting with a terrestrial pattern is called for.

In mid-summer during warm and sunny days, trout are inclined to lay-up in such areas especially if they offer shade. Such trout are not basically on a feeding station, but they choose a 'change of pace' zone to rest from the main current. Although not actively feeding the trout is fully aware that such locations often result in delectable terrestrial delicacies being on offer. Opportunities are seldom missed in the animal kingdom!

The angler must always carefully consider what natural terrestrial might be on offer in such locations. Ask yourself the questions, are leaf hoppers or caterpillars likely to fall off foliage? Are grass hoppers in that long grass? Are there many beetles on that earthern bank?

Having chosen a terrestrial offering that may naturally be seen at the location being fished, we must now consider how it might behave to appear natural.

Unlike aquatic flies, terrestrials find themselves on the water by dint of an accident. They fall, or are blown by the wind. We must try to simulate the accident that might have happened to our imitation at the location being fished.

Finding the right location is 30 per cent of the battle, choosing the right pattern is a further 20 per cent and the presentation is the final 50 per cent that clinches the victory.

14

Dry Fly v Damp Fly

All flyfishers have heard of dry flies and wet flies, but what, you might ask, is a damp fly? It is an expression I have chosen to describe a fly that is resting *in* the water surface film, (sometimes referred to as the meniscus).

The standard dry fly rests *on* the surface supported by the hackle points and sometimes the tail. Ideally the hook point and the fly body are supported above the water level.

Most, but not all, dry fly 'aficionados' maintain that in the above manner a light-pattern, (i.e. a pattern of sparkling pin-points of light), is created by the hackle points and is obvious to the fish before the actual fly is seen. The underwater surface always appears to the fish as a mirror reflecting the underwater environment. Therefore the actual standard fly cannot be seen, but the light pattern is visible in the mirror. The fly itself only becomes visible as it crosses Snell's Circle, (a prismatic ring), and enters the trout's viewing window. See Figs. 23 and 24.

In the case of the damp fly (see Fig. 22) the hook point, tail and body of the fly are fully visible in the undersurface mirror *before* it enters the viewing window. Unlike the dry fly, which when seen in the viewing window is just a hazy impression, the damp fly can be very clearly seen.

It is generally maintained that it is the light-pattern seen in the undersurface mirror that triggers the reaction for the fish to rise. It is believed that the rise actually commences to the light-pattern long before the fly is seen in the viewing window.

There is an old saying that 'there is no smoke without fire', and basically we must all accept the above theory as proven fact. However, this theory is only a small part of the story.

Firstly it must be appreciated that the viewing window varies in size depending on the swimming depth of the fish. See Figs. 23, 24 and 25. It also travels with the fish at all times. A fish on the feed just a few inches below the surface has a very small viewing window. As the fish floats back and rises the viewing window becomes even

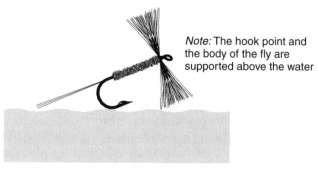

Note: The hook point and the body of the fly are supported above the water

Standard Dry Fly

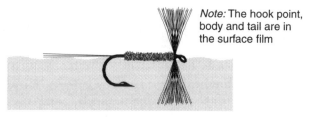

Note: The hook point, body and tail are in the surface film

The Damp Fly

Fig. 22   Dry and Damp Flies

smaller and moves back with the fish. See Fig. 15.

A fish on the stream-bed, possibly at a depth between 10in and 30in, has quite a large viewing window, but one that diminishes as the fish rises. See Fig. 25.

Our second point is that a light-pattern may well be clearly visible when a dry fly is resting on still water. It may be equally visible when being carried along an almost unbroken surface of a chalk stream. However, on a semi-turbulent small stream with plenty of surface ripple it is extremely doubtful that the rise is triggered by a light-pattern.

We will go further. A fish lying close to the stream-bed, with a large viewing window is hardly on the look-out for a light-pattern amongst the surface ripples.

After fishing the dry fly for over 40 years I am always impressed with the speed a trout rises in a small stream, particularly when compared to a stillwater or chalk stream trout.

I venture the opinion that this is due to the fact that the

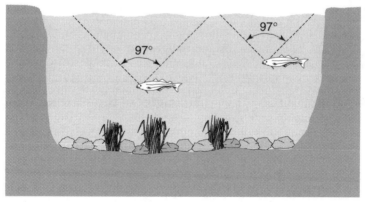

Note: The diminished viewing window at the higher position

Fig. 23   The Trout Window

93

The Small Stream Dry Fly

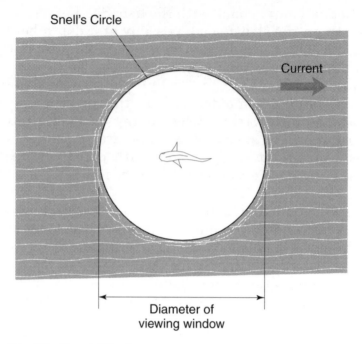

Fig. 24   *The Trout Window*

Depth of fish	Diameter of the Viewing Window
6in	1ft 2in
12in	2ft 3in
24in	4ft 6in
36in	6ft 10in
48in	9ft 1in

Fig. 25   *Trout at depth*

first sight of the fly is obtained in the viewing window and the rise commenced from depth.

Throughout these pages we have advocated using such flies as spent spinners, Klinkhamers, trimmed Grey Dusters and RF flies. *All* are flies that rest *in* the water surface. None of these flies creates the light-pattern of a standard dry fly. *They are all fished damp.* More important, they are all excellent takers of fish.

As a result of the above thoughts, two very important points emerge. (1) On a semi-turbulent small stream it is probably not essential, (and perhaps even not possible), to create a light-pattern. (2) When a fly is fished 'damp' it is often clearly seen by a deep lying fish as it passes through a larger viewing window.

We must bear these points in mind, and appreciate that the closer scrutiny that is possible of damp flies requires the flytier to pay more attention to detail. Fly shape, size and colour are important, and even more so are the materials used. Most aquatic flies have transluscent bodies so the dubbing should be kept sparse and the colour very carefully chosen. Always remember that a fish has an excellent view of a damp fly, albeit at times only a fleeting view, and we must insist that all flies to be fished damp are of very good quality.

15

Success or Failure

Most flyfishers measure success or failure by the number of fish caught. Some, fortunately only a few, by the size of the fish caught. Others may consider the success or failure of forays against a particular fish, or a specific set of circumstances.

The fact is that we all have our own particular yardstick against which we measure our personal success or failure.

Some years ago I used to fish with a Canadian friend who made a habit of breaking his flies at the hook-bend. He didn't de-barb his flies – he had no bend or barb! When a fish took his fly he maintained the game was over, he had deceived and outwitted the fish. He used to say 'There is no point in dragging the fish through the water to unhook it, I have already won the contest'. Few of us would want to follow this example, but it does make a point.

Most of us would not consider the game over and won until the fish was actually 'landed', but does that mean that the fish needs to physically leave the water? Could 'landed' also be interpreted as 'brought to the point of release'?

All of this brings us to the point of discussing catch and release . . .

Catch and Release

The case for 'catch and release', as far as the small stream flyfisher pursuing wild brown trout is concerned, may be best presented by considering the following scenario.

If a two mile stretch of river or stream has an average of one or two anglers on the water most days of the season, (between May and September, *i.e.* approx. 20 weeks), then there would have been a total of between 140 and 280 anglers fishing the water. Let us call it an average of 210 anglers. If each killed a brace of fish, then some 420 trout would be lost to the two mile stretch of river. No small stream without extensive replacement stocking programmes could afford such a cull.

However, even if the anglers do not actually kill the fish for the bag, the picture is possibly nearly as bleak through fish dying subsequent to being released.

We must also take into account the loss of fish through natural wastage.

All in all a frightening picture to contemplate. Is it a picture that demands 'catch and release'? Yes!, but it has to be 'catch and release' CORRECTLY CARRIED OUT.

The first step must be to study the hooks we use . . .

Hooks

Whether we intend to kill the trout we catch or to return them to the water, we should always seriously consider the use of barbless hooks. There are many advantages to a hook that is correctly made barbless, but the term 'barbless' is widely misunderstood. Little attention is usually paid to the actual de-barbing process.

The main reason for using a barbless hook is to avoid damage to the fish when unhooking. A second reason is that a barbless hook penetrates much more easily on the

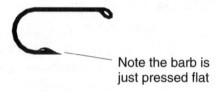

Note the barb is
just pressed flat

Angler de-barbed

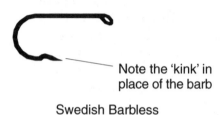

Note the 'kink' in
place of the barb

Swedish Barbless

Note the flat 'spade'
in place of the barb

Roman Moser Barbless

Fig. 26   Barbless Hooks

strike. There is a further reason, the hook on penetration makes a much smaller hole that is not likely to enlarge and loosen the hook hold as the fish fights for freedom. So, whether or not the fish is to be killed we have very definite advantages if we use barbless hooks.

However, as mentioned above, the hook needs to be made barbless in a correct manner. If we study the manufactured barbless hooks we will see that, in most cases, the absent barb has been replaced with another feature. Almost none of these hooks have plain needle points. See Fig. 26. True, the barb has been omitted but a small 'hump', 'kink' or 'spade' shape has replaced it. In this manner a firm hold on the fish is retained, but removal does not tear fish tissue.

If we de-barb our own hooks we only need to lightly press the barb down so that a 'hump' remains. Do not use a file, stone or hone to produce a needle point.

Failure to observe these points will often result in injured and dying fish, whether or not we return them to the water – in other words, *our initial success has been turned to failure.*

Let us now consider another way our initial success can be spoilt . . .

Releasing Captured Fish

If we intend to release a captured fish successfully we must observe and follow established guidelines:

1. The fish must be brought to release as quickly as possible. Every minute the fish fights for freedom its chance of survival is diminished. The energy expended, plus the trauma, takes a toll on the system and internal organs.

2. The fish must not be out of the water for more than 30 seconds. Time spent on the bank being admired and photographed causes damage to the gills.

3. The fish must be handled as little as possible. Try not to handle a fish at all, it may damage the covering mucus on the body. Always wet your hands well before touching. Try to unhook the fish whilst it is in the net using a release tool or forceps. Return the fish to the water while it is still in the net.

4. Do not lay the netted fish down on the bank, because damage can be done to the covering mucus by the fish coming into contact with dirt, sand or gravel.

Note: All these guidelines can be fully observed by the excellent practice of using a release tool, (Ketchum Release or similar), whilst the fish is still in the water.

We can now turn our attention to a further way we are able to turn initial success into failure . . .

Faulty Tackle

Many anglers take immense pride in their tackle. Hours are spent on caring for it, servicing it and just lovingly admiring it. Others adopt a 'macho' approach – all items of tackle are just tools to be used and then thrown loose into a car boot.

It is your tackle, you are entitled to treat it as you like but never forget it can be the cause of a miserable failure after you have done everything else correctly.

The most frequent cause of failure is a dragging fly brought about by a poorly floating flyline. A flyline that has partially sunk into the water surface film is far more susceptible to the vagaries of the current. A neglected flyline picks up dirt and scum that not only damages rod-rings by abrasion but also causes minute cracking of the line coating and lets in water. The hydrophobic coating of the line (a water repellent) is also damaged.

All of the above can be avoided by a few minutes' attention. At the end of a day's fishing wipe the flyline with a soapy wet cloth, wipe dry with a paper towel then every third time fishing rub in a little line dressing. Not only will your fishing improve but you will save money on flylines.

Another cause for failure is a badly maintained reel. Although it seems hard to believe, I have on three separate occasions witnessed an angler have his reel drop off the rod and into the water whilst playing a fish! Only on one occasion did the reel fall out of the rod reel-seat, the other two times the spool fell out of the reel.

A reel is an expensive and purely mechanical item. It should be a treasured item. Like all mechanical devices it requires regular inspection and maintenance, (cleaning and oiling), and don't forget to inspect the rod reel-seat from time to time!

Elsewhere in these pages we have mentioned leaders and nylon knots. Both can turn a triumphant success into an abject failure. However, never forget that such failure is entirely our own fault. Inspection of nylon for signs of wear, and the correct type of knots, is in our own hands. Also, throw away nylon from last season that has been exposed to hours of sunlight, it cannot be trusted enough for our needs.

Some Final Thoughts

Instead of 'final thoughts' we might have used a heading of 'common sense'.

It is useless honing our technique to a high standard if

we act in a robotic manner and fail to use basic common sense.

It is simply beyond understanding to see an angler presenting a fly beautifully when, because of a lack of vision enhancement, he/she can't see the fly on the water. Polaroid sunglasses plus side-shields are, more often than not, essential to see our flies correctly.

It is a peculiar fact that when the predominant light is from a certain direction the water surface appears to be a silver/grey colour and our flies just simply disappear from view. Polaroid glasses tinted yellow overcome this particular problem, although they are not too helpful under other conditions. It is one of the reasons that I carry more than one pair of polaroids, I wouldn't be without them.

Attention to these details, plus many others, is just plain common sense. We all become blasé at times and inclined to overlook the finer points of preparation – to our cost.

Moments of triumph are to be treasured and should never be turned into dismal failure when it can be avoided.

Appendix 'A'

The 'Change of Pace' Zones

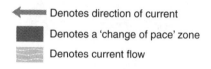

Denotes direction of current

Denotes a 'change of pace' zone

Denotes current flow

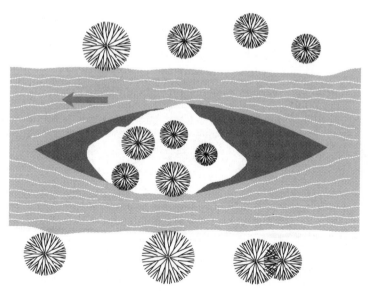

(1) The mid-stream island

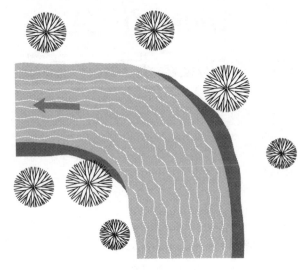

(2) River bend

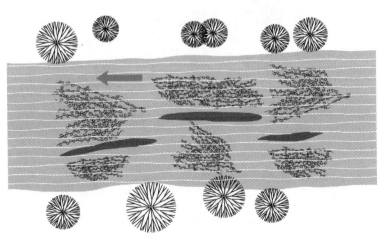

(3) Weedbed channels

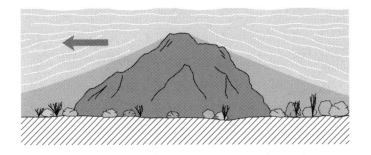

(4) Underwater rock

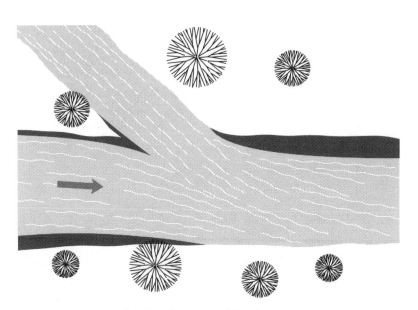

(5) Confluence with tributary

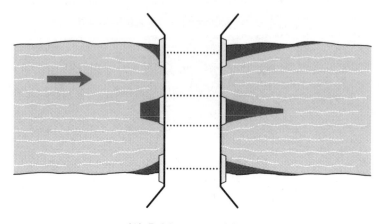

(6) Bridge stanchions

(7) River weir

The 'Change of Pace' Zones

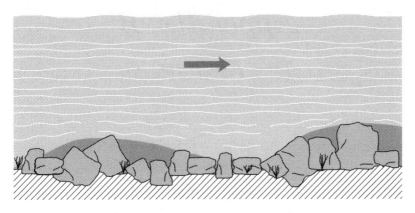

(8) Rocky stream bed

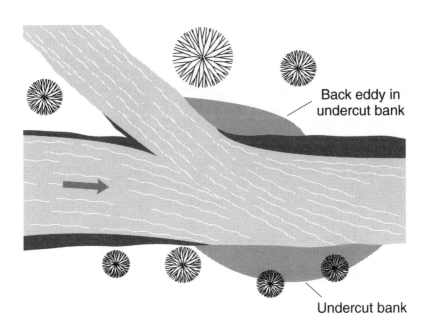

Back eddy in
undercut bank

Undercut bank

(9) Confluence with tributary

Appendix 'B'

Dry Fly Patterns

DARK OLIVE
Hook: 14
Silk: Olive
Tail: Dark olive
Body: Olive dubbing
Rib: White floss
Hackle: Blue dun and olive

LARGE RED SPINNER
Hook: 12 to 14
Silk: Claret
Tail: Red cock
Body: Claret dubbing
Rib: Gold wire
Hackle: Red cock

BLUE UPRIGHT
Hook: 14
Silk: Black
Tail: Blue dun
Body: Peacock eye quill
Rib: None
Hackle: Medium blue dun

MEDIUM OLIVE
Hook: 16
Silk: Green
Tail: Blue dun
Body: Olive hackle stalk
Rib: None
Hackle: Pale ginger

GOLD RIBBED HARE'S EAR
Hook: 14 or 16
Silk: Yellow
Tail: Body strands
Body: Hare's ear dubbing
Rib: Flat gold tinsel
Hackle: Dubbing picked out

GREENWELL'S GLORY
Hook: 14
Silk: Yellow
Tail: Furnace
Body: Waxed tying silk
Rib: Gold wire
Hackle: Furnace

Dry Fly Patterns

LUNN'S PARTICULAR
Hook: 14 or 16
Silk: Crimson
Tail: Red
Body: Red hackle stalk
Rib: None
Hackle: Red and blue dun

PALE WATERY
Hook: 14 or 16
Silk: Primrose
Tail: Cream
Body: Heron herl
Rib: None
Hackle: Cream

BLUE WINGED OLIVE (B.W.O.)
Hook: 14
Silk: Orange
Tail: Olive
Body: Olive ostrich herl
Rib: None
Hackle: Blue dun or olive

AMBER SPINNER
Hook: 14
Silk: White
Tail: Cree
Body: Orange floss
Rib: Brown silk
Hackle: Blue dun

SHERRY SPINNER
Hook: 14 or 16
Silk: Orange
Tail: Light ginger
Body: Orange floss
Rib: Gold wire
Hackle: Red

IRON BLUE
Hook: 14 or 16
Silk: Purple
Tail: White
Body: Pheasant tail herl
Rib: None
Hackle: Slate

TUP'S INDISPENSABLE
Hook: 16
Silk: Yellow
Tail: Blue dun
Body: Tup mixture, silk at rear
Rib: None
Hackle: Blue dun

HOUGHTON RUBY
Hook: 14
Silk: Crimson
Tail: White
Body: Red hackle stalk
Rib: None
Hackle: Red and blue dun

The Small Stream Dry Fly

JENNY SPINNER
Hook: 14 or 16
Silk: Crimson
Tail: White
Body: Magenta dubbing
Rib: Crimson silk
Hackle: Slate

ALDER
Hook: 10 or 12
Silk: Yellow
Tail: None
Body: Pheasant tail
Rib: None
Hackle: Blue dun

MARCH BROWN
Hook: 12
Silk: Primrose
Tail: Cree
Body: Hare's ear
Rib: Yellow silk
Hackle: Cree

BI-VISIBLE
Hook: 12 to 16
Silk: To suit hackle
Tail: Two hackle tips
Body: Tying silk
Rib: None
Hackle: To suit/white in front

SILVER SEDGE
Hook: 12 or 14
Silk: Grey
Tail: None
Body: Grey dubbing
Rib: Silver wire
Wing: Grey duck
Hackle: Ginger palmered

GRIFFITH'S GNAT
Hook: 18 to 24
Silk: Black
Tail: None
Body: Peacock herl
Rib: Nil
Hackle: Grizzle palmered

GREY DUSTER
Hook: 14 to 18
Silk: Black
Tail: Silver badger
Body: Grey dubbing
Rib: None
Hackle: Silver badger

WELSHMAN'S BUTTON
Hook: 12 or 14
Silk: Brown
Tail: None
Body: Turkey fibre/yellow silk in centre
Rib: Nil
Wing: Turkey
Hackle: Red palmered

KLINKHAMER
Hook: 12
Silk: Brown
Tail: None
Body: Hare's ear dubbing
Thorax: Peacock herl
Wing: White synthetic yarn
Hackle: Blue dun tied parachute

Further Reading

Flyfishing – Tactics on Small Streams (Swan Hill Press)
Lou Stevens

A Modern Dry Fly Code (Crown Publishers Inc. NY)
Vincent Marinaro

What The Trout Said (Swan Hill Press) Datus Proper

Trout and Terrestrials (Swan Hill Press) Lou Stevens

Micro Patterns (Swan Hill Press) Darrel Martin

Index

Index